Y0-BRQ-327

For Cardinal Fans Only

Volume II

by Rich Wolfe

Published by Lone Wolfe Press, a division of Richcraft. Distribution, marketing, publicity, interviews, and book signings handled by Wolfegang Marketing Systems, Ltd.—But Not Very.

This book is not affiliated with or endorsed by the St. Louis Cardinals or MLB.

Photo Credits:
    Craig Ball, St. Louis
    Don Marquess, KMOX Photos

Layout: The Printed Page, Phoenix, AZ
Author's agent: T. Roy Gaul

Rich Wolfe can be reached at 602-738-5889

ISBN: 978-0-9846278-8-2

DEDICATION

To
Steve Sabol
1942-2012
NFL Films

Neat man, fun guy, wonderful friend

CHAT ROOMS

PREFACE

Bless me Cardinal fans, for I have sinned. It has been many years since my last confession. In 2002, I did a book called *Remembering Jack Buck* which at the time became the bestselling book in the history of the Cardinals. The next year brought *For Cardinal Fans Only,* a book that was very well received. In fact, at the Cardinals Winter Warm-Up the following January, Cardinal historian Erv Fischer said that he had read every book ever written about the Cardinals and he considered that book the best ever. To this day, a total of almost four dozen books later, I have never had a compliment that meant more to me.

In the interim...I did four books on the Chicago Cubs. Jack Buck called the Cubs-Cardinals rivalry the best in sports because of the fans' civility. Cubs fans and the Cubs management were quite enjoyable. That's my confession. The spirit was willing, and the flesh was weak.

There are a couple offshoots of the first Cardinal book that are worth mentioning. In 1978, during the midst of a huge blizzard, my brother-in-law and I played Scrabble one Christmas Eve well into Christmas morning. We're both very competitive, and it came down to the very last letters. There was money changing hands and we also were having some liquid fortification against the unknown.

I had a slight lead on my brother-in-law...with three letters left—a "Q", a "G", and a "U". There was no place to use those letters which meant the points were going to be subtracted from my score. My brother-in-law would win the game, bragging rights, and the $20.

On the lower left side of the board going downward to the left-hand corner was the word "PATCH". Those three letters fit nicely above the word "patch," forming the word "QUGPATCH" which was also a triple word score. It was no surprise that my brother-in-law began making more noise than a stuck pig. He went crazy and woke up the whole house. "What is that word?" "That is what you use to fill a leak in a qug." He went ballistic! By this time, everyone is awake in the house. Finally, he said, "I am not paying you, and I will not pay you until the day you show me that word in writing."

It is not a surprise that he is no longer my brother-in-law and hasn't been in several decades. On the other hand, in 2003 while doing *For Cardinal Fans Only*, inspiration struck! There was a wonderful interview with *his* brother-in-law on page 157 of the book. The headline says, "A Qugpatch Is What It Was". He was sent the book with a note that said, "Fast pay makes fast friends."

The same year I did a book called *For Red Sox Fans Only* that became quite successful. Early in the spring of 2004, I received a call from a Los Angeles production company that was working on "Fever Pitch". "Fever Pitch" is a movie that originally was going to star Matt Damon, but ended up starring Jimmy Fallon and Drew Barrymore. The essence of the story was that Jimmy Fallon's character was a huge Red Sox fan, Drew Barrymore knew nothing about baseball when they started dating. The idea of the producer was that they would be together in a bookstore and suddenly, Fallon's character would spy *For Red Sox Fans Only*, pick it up, hand it to her and say, "If you want to understand what Red Sox fans are all about, read this book and then you'll know. It's a great book!" The producer's assistant wanted to know if that would be okay. She said, "We will invite you to Toronto where we're going to film the scene so you can be a technical advisor."

That meant there was going to be tremendous demand for the Red Sox book, which had already sold out. Another 20,000 Sox books were ordered and the printer was ready to print perhaps double that number depending on how the movie did.

The movie came out on a Friday. Through the whole movie there was no sight of any bookstore scene. On Monday I called the production company in Los Angeles, talked to the producer's assistant and said, "Hey! Were there two versions of this movie?" Meanwhile, there were 20,000 books sitting in a warehouse ready to be shipped. She said, "Oh! I should have told you. When we started the movie, we never dreamed that the Red Sox would win the World Series, but we went to St. Louis, filmed and added scenes the night they actually won the World Series." I told her, "I was there for those two games in St. Louis. I've been a Cardinal fan twice as long as you've been alive. This is a double disaster."

The bottom line is, if any of you are Red Sox fans or know Red Sox fans, and would like a very nice price on a Red Sox book, let me know. As a matter of fact, just jot your name, address and credit card number on the back of a $20 bill and send it along...much obliged.

Anyway, here we go again. Please absolve me of these Cubs sins so we can get to this Cardinal book with quite a different title. You should know that I'm an old man and not really an author even though I've done 47 books, can't type and have never turned on a computer.

Since the age of ten, I've been a serious collector of sports books. During that time—for the sake of argument, let's call it 30 years—my favorite book style is the eavesdropping type where the subject talks in his or her own words—without the "then he said" or "the air was so thick you could cut it with a butter knife" waste of verbiage that makes is so hard to get the meat of the matter. Books such as Lawrence Ritter's *Glory of Their Times* and Donald Honig's *Baseball When the Grass Was Real.* Thus, that style was adopted when I started compiling oral histories of the Jack Bucks and Harry Carays of the world. I'm a sports fan first and foremost—I don't even pretend to be an author. This book is designed solely for other Cardinal fans. I really don't care what the publisher, editors or critics think—only that Cardinals fans have an enjoyable read and get their money's worth. Sometimes a person being interviewed will drift off the subject but if the feeling is that Cardinals fans would enjoy the digression, it stays in the book.

In an effort to get more material into the book, the editor decided to merge some paragraphs and alter some punctuation, which will allow for the reader to receive an additional 10,000 words, the equivalent of 25 pages. More bang for your buck...more fodder for English teachers...fewer dead trees.

Hopefully the stories you are about to read will bring back even more wonderful memories of your youth and your Cardinal fandom. We are all circling the drain faster everyday, but if the Lord is willing and the creek don't rise, we'll have more Cardinal books for you in the future. To quote Mr. Bartles and Mr. James, "Thank you for your support."

Go now.

Rich Wolfe

Falmouth, Massachusetts

Chapter One

GROWIN' UP
A CARDINAL

12 Years Old Forever

BASEBALL MEMORIES ARE FREE AND WORTH EVERY PENNY

GREG MARECEK

Greg Marecek has been in the sports business for 35 years, serving as a sportswriter and editor, sportscaster, national sports syndicator, and sports radio owner. He is a member of the Missouri Sports Hall of Fame. An avid, lifelong collector of sports memorabilia, his latest project is a beautiful book called The Cardinals of Cooperstown.

I met Joe Cunningham and Don Blasingame as a little boy— it was exciting! My dad and I were out for lunch. They gave me autographed pictures, which I still have to this day. One day, Bill White and Charlie James came to Webster Groves and signed at a local store, called "Robert's Boys Shop." I had won an award which gave me the opportunity to go over there to meet them. Charlie James is a Webster Groves native, so that made it even better. I was in third grade at the time.

I'm a sports collector, so I have hundreds of autographed balls, pennants and scorecards. I was a collector from the beginning. A lot of kids were getting the "penny packs" and buying little cards. They would play "flips" with them or they would put the cards in their bicycle spokes. I had two rules: I never put them in my bicycle spokes and I would only flip them if they were duplicates because I was going to keep the collection. Consequently to this day, I have all of the baseball cards that TOPPS made from 1955 to 1960…the full sets.

In those days...back in '55, **TOPPS*** only put out eight player cards per team. If you look at those 1955, '56, and '57 sets, you will see there are far less cards than there were players in the league at the time. Stan wasn't in some of those sets, as I was told, because he felt he wasn't being paid enough money for them. So he missed some series. However, when he was in the cards, for some reason, I was able to collect him pretty easily. Now I have a number of Stan Musial cards that are worth a fair amount of money....$300, $400, or $500 each. It depends on the year and they have to be in great condition, but they are definitely worth that much.

I always loved collecting Kenny Boyer cards. When I was in the first grade, I had a Cisco Kid lunch box. My great teacher, Miss McClain, knew about my interest in baseball. She said to me, "You like cards. I know that you're sitting at your desk with some of them in your pocket all of the time. Would you like to bring your cards in for the whole class to see?" I went home and told my mom and she let me fill my Cisco Kid lunch box with all of my cards. It was packed with three rows. I brought them into class, and opened it up like you were opening up a bag of money. I went through all of the cards. She was amazed at the interest that I had at age seven. The other kids barely knew what baseball cards were and didn't have much interest. And now...if they had collected them back then, they would have money...a lot of money!

When I became a sportswriter, nobody cared about autographs, everybody signed everything. The Cardinals used to

*Bob Uecker said he knew his career was over in 1965 when his baseball card came out without his picture on it. **TOPPS** has made many mistakes with their baseball cards over the years. In 1956, Hank Aaron's picture of sliding into home plate was actually Willie Mays. The next year, Aaron is shown batting left handed because the negative was reversed. In 1969, catcher Larry Haney showed up as a left-handed catcher because his negative was also reversed.

have these Old Timers games and most of the time it would be the National League Old Timers against the American League Old Timers. The Cardinals would bring in all of these old retired players—just unbelievable names. They would play for three innings before a Cardinal game. At one of these games, there was a former player that was then 75 years old who hit a home run into the bleachers—at 75 years old! Luke Appling. The Cardinals didn't care if you were a reporter, or whoever you were, they said, "If you could get an autograph...go get it!" I would always carry a ball in my pocket so that I could get it autographed. I did all of the Old Timers Games. I went into the American League dugout and handed a ball to Casey Stengel. He said, "Hey listen, how about I sign it and pass it down?" He took the pen and signed it, then passed it to **MICKEY MANTLE*** who passed it to Whitey Ford, who then passed it to Joe DiMaggio and Joe did sign it, by the way. It went right on down the line.

I used to listen to the games on a little crystal set in my own little bedroom. My mom would say, "Go to sleep" and my dad would say, "Let him listen to the ballgame, he'll go to sleep." I would listen to the game through a little headset, listening to Harry, Jack and Joe. It was awesome.

*Martha Stewart often was the babysitter for Yogi Berra and **MICKEY MANTLE**'s kids in the early '60s.

WHERE THE PAST IS PRESENT

JEFF BELL

Jeff Bell, originally from Cahokia, Illinois now lives in Columbia, Illinois. Bell, a teacher, made the Southern Illinois University baseball team in college, but never played because of a hockey injury. He now plays in the MSBL (Men's Senior Baseball League).

I actually have a piece of Sportsman's Park. I have the big Cardinal Bird, the 4'x4' Cardinal Bird. After August Busch took over, they revamped the Park and put a press box up there on top—behind home plate. It was on top of the roof. There were five different poses of Cardinal birds on the press box. They were 4'x4' metal birds, and I got the one that was all the way on the third base side. It was a Cardinal batting, getting ready to hit. Whoever tore down the Park had a storage place right there underneath the MacArthur Bridge, which was the main way to get into downtown in those days. I found the Cardinal Bird there.

Sportman's Park had closed down and they had the pieces of the park there. I could never get my dad to stop. When I started working and making my own money, I stopped by after work one day in my '68 Pontiac and asked the guy how much he wanted for the Cardinal Bird. He said he wanted ten bucks. I told him that I didn't have ten bucks, that I only had $7.50. He said, "I'll take it!" So I brought it home and I still have it today.

When I brought it home, my dad asked me, "What in the heck are you going to do with that?" I said, "I don't know? Maybe when I get my own place, I'll put it up and display it somehow?" I have it in my basement now and I'm getting ready to build my man-cave so I'll put it up there. I have a couple of postcards where you can see the Cardinal sign. You could really tell it's the sign I got. I'll be able to pass it down to my kids....

We ended up getting a partial season ticket in '78. Back then it wasn't that crowded at Busch Stadium; there would only be fifteen to twenty thousand people there. We would wait by the players' exit after the game. My wife's favorite player was Ted Simmons and since I was a catcher, I would go talk to him after the game. We would talk to Lou Brock for awhile and Ken Reitz would always come out and talk to the fans. Ted Simmons got to the point where he knew Kathy and I and he would just say, "Hey! What's up?" The players would just come out, stop and sign, go over to the parking garage and go home—not like today where they aren't as available. We might have to wait an hour or so. Simmons knew that I played ball, and he would ask me how my season was going and I would always say, "Not as good as yours!" He always gave me some tips on catching too. He was just a nice guy and always had time for his fans. Oh my gosh—that guy could hit! I don't know how many times he would hit line drives that were caught in center field or caught at the top of the wall that would have been doubles? He was just an exceptional hitter! He had to go up against Johnny Bench who was always getting the press back then because he was with the Big Red Machine. The Cardinals always had great hitting in the '70's, they just didn't have pitching. They would lose games 8-7—it was frustrating....

During the '82 World Series, I was lucky to go to Game 7. That was pretty cool, but I was by myself. I couldn't get any more tickets because one of the salesmen where I worked had gotten me just the one ticket. After that Series, was when they tore all of the turf out and put the new stuff in. During the day games, when a ground ball was hit, you couldn't see where the ground ball was, especially on TV! I got a big piece of the Astroturf and it cost $80. It's a 25x20 section and I still have it underneath a glass case in my man-cave.

I also have a couple of the seats when they tore them out to put in the new ones. They were putting the plastic seats in huge bins—they were going to recycle them. One day it was about six o'clock in the morning—just before I took off on my work route—where I worked wasn't too far from the Stadium so I figured that I would grab some of the seats. I climbed into this huge, long dumpster. These dumpsters were 20-25 feet long and eight feet wide. They were filled with seats!! You could just go pick any one of them out. I started picking some out and there was this guy there with a produce truck from Breese, Illinois. He tells me, "You need to match the seats; there are numbers on the sides. You have to look for a "20 and a 20" or a "21 and a 21." You have to match the backs with the bottoms." I asked him, "How do you know?" He said, "We're replacing all of our seats in Breese with these plastic ones." They have a nice little Montclair ballpark there in Breese. I said, "Oh, you're replacing the old seats you have there?" He said, "Yeah, the old ones are seats that we got from the old Sportsman's Park years ago." I said, "Oh, for crying out loud! If you're going to replace them, can you bring me in a couple?" He said, "I sure will!" So that's how I got my seats from Sportsman's Park! I should have gone over to Breese to get more of them because now they're wanting $100.00 a seat!

I remember when I got the seats. They were doing major construction and they were putting bins of the metal legs in the parking lot right next to the Stadium. I stopped by and told the guy that was out there that I had got the seats from the bins and asked him if they were selling the legs or if they were throwing them away too. He said, "No. We're shipping them off to get repainted and we're bringing them back to re-use them." He said, "You know, sometimes when we try to take them apart, some of them break, so we have to replace them anyway. How many seats do you have?" I told him that I had twelve and he said, "Well, I don't know if you can have that many, but I'm going to go eat lunch and I'm the only one here...so if some of them disappear, I don't think we're going to notice them missing." Then he said, "If they do happen to disappear, you need to make sure you have a left side, a right side and the ones in between!" I thought that was pretty cool! He was basically telling me to go ahead and take some of the legs! I said, "Okay! Thanks!"...

My brother and I went to the old ballpark on Thanksgiving in '74—old Sportsman's Park. My brother was living in Washington, D.C. but was in St. Louis at the time. He said, "Let's go over to Sportsman's Park to see if it's still there. Let's take some balls and gloves." We took our little brother with us and we went over to Sportsman's Park. It was a cold, bitter day. The infield was still the way it was before—I mean it was still all cut out. The pitcher's mound was still a mound. Home plate was a perfect circle and the baselines were all there but the grass was a little bit longer. Obviously, there were no stands there but you could make out where the dugouts were. The foul lines were still there. They weren't chalked, but where the chalk was for so many years, there was no grass. So we followed the foul line to where it just dead ended where the right or left field corner would be. We went out there and were playing on the field for about an hour until we got too cold to play anymore. We were standing there batting and saying, "Jeepers! This is where **BABE RUTH*** stood...this is where Lou Gehrig stood and Stan the Man! **HANK AARON*** stood here and Mickey Mantle was here in the '64 World Series!" You also have to remember the Browns were there up until '53 so all of the American League players had played there too. It was really cool being able to

***BABE RUTH** stole home fifteen times....In Babe Ruth's first major league game—as a pitcher for the Boston Red Sox—he was removed in the 7th inning for a pinch hitter.

*Denny's famous Grand Slam Breakfast was introduced in 1977 in Atlanta to honor **HANK AARON**.

stand in the same spots. We were throwing off the spot where Gibson was pitching in the World Series. I just wish my kids had been born then so I they could have been there with me!

My older brother and I had a hankering for the old Sportsman's Park. After the mid-sixties all of the new stadiums were round and they were used for football, soccer and baseball and they didn't have as much character to them as the old ball parks did. I remember the one game that we did go to at Sportsman's Park. We couldn't find a place to park, so we parked on a side street off of Grand. My dad said, "Make sure you stick close." I noticed the area was not very good up there on the North Side. He made sure to park under a street light as well. When you're a kid, you think it's neat when you hear that they're building a new stadium, but it's also sad to see the old park go. I remember when they flew the home plate from the old park over to the new one in a helicopter. I saw it on TV. That was really cool!

I recall it being really hot when the **1966*** All-Star Game was in town. We were sitting in our non-air conditioned house watching it. Tim McCarver scored the winning run. That was back when the starters would play and they might bat three or four times because they were actually trying to win. Mays had a base hit driving in Timmy McCarver, which I thought was pretty cool. I do remember the line-up from that game because I was getting older and getting more appreciative of baseball players. Al Kaline, Harmon Killebrew, Tony Oliva, Koufax, Drysdale...all of those guys were in the lineup. Of course, Gibson, McCarver, and I'm pretty sure Lou Brock were both there. When you think about that year and how many of those guys are in the Hall of Fame now it's just amazing!

*In **1966**, Busch Stadium opened at a cost of 25 million dollars. In 2006, the new Busch opened at a cost of 345 million dollars. Fenway cost $300,000 to build in 1912 and Wrigley Field $250,000 in 1914.

The site of Sportsman's Park as it looked in 2011

I was lucky to grow up in that era. There weren't that many teams, but every team had at least **THREE GOOD PITCHERS*** on it. And the teams that had four good pitchers were even tougher. So anybody that batted .300 back then was just a really good hitter. It was before specialty pitching. Pitchers just pitched.

*One out of every eight of Mike Shannon's at bats in the Big Leagues was against a Hall of Fame PITCHER.

BUSCH STADIUM:
THE LAST REFUGE OF SCOUNDRELS

KATHLEEN LANGLEY

In 1982, Kathleen Langley crafted a Cardinal collectible magnet out of a peanut, a pipe cleaner, googly eyes and a toothpick that ended up on most Cardinal fans' refrigerators. This creativity lead her to eventually open the craft boutique, Little House on Prairie, *in the town of Greenfield, Illinois where she still lives.*

When the Stadium first opened in 1966, my dad started working at the Stadium in the concession stand. There were six kids in my family. Some of us would actually go with my dad to work. Usually it was me, my brother and sister, but there were other kids from the neighborhood that went with us at times. At that time we lived in Cahokia, so it wasn't that far of a trip. Since he had to be there so many hours before the game, we would walk with him to a certain point until he had to put his uniform on, and then we would wait outside by the press gate.

We would stand outside the Stadium, waiting until the gates opened. Dad knew the usher who worked that gate. We would wait outside the gate, and once it was clear, his friend would let us sneak under the turnstile. I was nine at the time. We would watch the players as they came in. It seems like we were right above where they actually came in on the ground floor. They were dressed up, looking nice. People were always watching, "Oh, there's Lou Brock...and there's Tim McCarver." You could always tell the way they were decked out with their nice clothes that the players were coming in whether it was from the other team or a Cardinal. Our team was always looking dapper.

When we finally got inside the Stadium, we would have a seat wherever we wanted until somebody came along with their ticket stubs and said, "I think you're in our seats?" We were like, "Ohhhh, we're sorry" and then we would move somewhere else. We would do that until the game started or until we found seats that nobody was claiming, and then we stayed there to watch the game. We probably went to every home game, and got to watch players like **ORLANDO CEPEDA*,** Bob Gibson, Tim McCarver, Lou Brock, Curt Flood. We were not allowed to wander too far out from the concession stand where my dad worked at the time, so we weren't able to run all over the Stadium. There was a time when he actually worked in the concession stand over by the bleachers. At the time, the bleacher seats were $1.00 and were first come, first serve so we didn't have to jump around seat to seat.

There were a lot of good times. Looking back, we went to so many games it was almost like we ended up getting burnt out because we had gone to so many—always jumping from seat to seat. That was actually pretty embarrassing because we were settled in, and then all of a sudden, here comes an usher with ticket stubs, "Uh, you're in their seats...can we see your tickets?"

One of the freebies that I can remember was a miniature baseball bat. It was a writing pen with the Cardinal logo on it. I always thought they were really cool. There were also little baseballs in little plastic containers. It looked like everybody had signed it but I'm sure it wasn't autographed by everybody—it was probably just a stamp.

People dressed up to go to the games more so at that time. Jeans were not a big to-do. Going to the game was more like

*__ORLANDO CEPEDA__ used more bats than any player in history. He felt each bat had exactly one hit in it. When Cepeda hit safely, he would discard the bat. He had 2,364 hits in his career.

they were going to the Fox Theater; people dressed up more. Even as kids, I don't remember wearing jeans to the game -we had on nice short sets. We didn't have a lot, but I know that we dressed more nicely to go than what you see today. It was nice to see the women dressed up, having on all of their jewelry, and the men were dressed up too. It was like a big outing for everyone!

The scoreboard was so amazing back then when they hit a home run. The way the lights were made it looked like a Cardinal bird was flying across the board. They didn't do fireworks back when I used to go, they just had the bird that flew across the board, tipped his hat and then went back and sat on the bat. That was great!

My sister was born on the day we won the '64 World Series. For some reason that I don't understand, my dad was working at the ball game that day and my mom was off having the baby. Even now, I don't know why he wasn't with her; maybe he couldn't get off, but I know they must have had special food that day! He brought home rolled roast beef. There were pieces of roast beef rolled and kept closed with a toothpick plus little cups of pickles and salad. I can just remember him coming home with these little cups of salad and condiments and this rolled roast beef. That's what we had for supper that night. That's how we celebrated the birth of my sister, Paula, in October of 1964, as well as the Cards winning the World Series that day!

FANECDOTES

When baseball season gets in full swing, it reminds me of a boy I used to be with all the time when I was growing up on a farm near Floris, Iowa. He was the most avid Cardinal fan I've had the pleasure to know. He would spend hours with an old stick, hitting rocks across a gravel road where he lived. It was always the Cardinals against the world—usually the **CUBS*** or the Yankees. He knew which way every batter for the Cardinals would swing. If the Cardinal was a left-handed hitter, that's how the boy would strike the rock. If he was right-handed, the boy would swing from the right hand side. He would play nine innings and the Cardinals always managed to stage a rally and win the game. When he was still a young man, his dad bought him a portable radio and he listened to every game the Cardinals played. When the Brooklyn Dodgers moved to Los Angeles and the New York Giants to San Francisco in 1958, there were a lot of late nights for the boy when the Cardinals were on the West Coast. If he wasn't listening to baseball, he was playing baseball. He even mowed the pasture with a lawn mower for the infield, mowed foul lines and built a backstop. Sometimes, the cows got in the way or left remnants that had to be avoided while playing, but the game always went on. His worst trait was he hated for the Cardinals to lose. There were some old-timers in town that loved to tease him about the Cardinals. They were always sitting in front of the grocery store or produce store and had names like Ace, Windy, Cranberry Merchant and Shug. They said you could always tell if the Cardinals won because the boy would come to town with a big grin on his face, but if the Cardinals lost you would never lay eyes on him. The boy always said Ace was his favorite because he was the only true Cardinal fan in the bunch. I always think about that boy when

*When Chicagoan Joe Davita, 78, died in 2001 his obituary read: "Memorials to **CUBS** so they can acquire a qualified relief pitcher."

the Cardinals open their season. He still hangs on every pitch, every hit and lives and dies with the Cardinals. If it was up to him, the Cardinal flag would be flying every day.

That little boy was me.

—**Ron Morgan**, Lancaster, MO

My Cardinal obsession as a little boy paid off in more ways than one. I learned to do math with Cardinal players' baseball cards and statistics in the Post-Dispatch. Figuring batting averages helped me a lot in my math classes. I only got to go to one game a year when I was a pre-teen. I always remember my one game, one year when we were playing the **BROOKLYN DODGERS***. They were killing us 13-1 but I wouldn't let my dad leave until the last out. He was not real happy about that. Hey, Wally Moon hit a home run, it wasn't all bad. The big payoff for my Cardinal love came one year soon after when the entire family bought tickets to a game and we left from uncle's house in south St. Louis. When we got to Sportsman's Park my parents discovered the tickets had been left back at my uncle's house. Major disaster. My one big chance of the year. It just couldn't happen. I tugged on my dad's shirt and proceeded to matter-of-factly spit out the section, row and set numbers of the tickets. They had let me hold the tickets back at the house and so I did, as if they were gold coins. My dad looked at me funny, took my hand and led our whole group over to the ticket taker. Dad explained what had happened and then gave me a nod. I repeated my details as serious as could be. The ticket man looked at my dad, looked at me, shook his head and let everybody in. Even the most somber little boy might have trouble pulling that off today, don't you think?

—**Jack Lovelace**, Fort Collins, Colorado

*Only 6,700 fans attended the **DODGERS**' finale at Ebbets Field in 1957. The park—built 44 years earlier—had a capacity of 32,000 with only 700 parking spaces. An apartment building now sits on that site.

I started listening to Cardinal baseball in the last half of the 1960s but didn't become a strong fan until I watched the 1967 World Series between the Cardinals and the Red Sox. I was 13 years old and in the 8th grade at Christ the King Catholic School in Fort Smith, Arkansas. The school had K–8 and everybody knew that the eighth graders were treated like seniors in high school. We got to do things like raise and lower the flag every day, ring the bell for recess and run the Coke machine at the 2 P.M. break. The eighth grade also had the only television out of all the other classes in the school. It just so happened that our teacher, Sister Mary Beatrice, was not only the principal but also an avid Red Sox fan. So, when a game was on, we would finish whatever subject we were doing and then we were allowed to watch a couple innings of the game. Back in 1967 all World Series games were still being played and broadcast in the afternoon so we had quite a few chances to watch some of the Series. I remember Bob Gibson hit a fifth inning, two-run homer in Game 7 and Sister Mary Beatrice felt that I had betrayed her.

—**Dave Weisenfels**, Fort Smith, Arkansas

Back when I was in grade school, they still had the straight-A student tickets. I don't know if they still do that anymore, but I always got them. We were at Sportsman's Park in about 1962 because we would have still been in grade school. At that time, kids rode on the bus downtown and our parents didn't worry about us. We had bus passes because we went to a Catholic school—we had to have bus passes to get to school every week. On the weekend, we would go all over St. Louis including the ballpark on our bus passes. I remember going with one of my friends and Stan Musial was pretty close to us. We kept yelling, "Stan! Stan!" My friend's grandparents were Polish so she yells out, "Stashu!" in Polish! He looked up and he waved at us! That was a really great time and we felt like we were really something special! And he was like, "How did you know?" I think it was "Stashu"...I don't know, it's been a long time...I can't really remember all of it? But I do remember, though, having him look straight at us—it was like having some god looking at us. Isn't that amazing that Stan was so good and you didn't see him running off to make more money somewhere.

The straight A seats were up at the top, but it was still free! I would take my daddy and his sister...she loved baseball! My dad's whole family...every time that we would get together with any of his family, it seemed like the **RADIO*** was on, baseball was playing, and everybody would sit around it. We all knew what was going on, we knew all the names of the players; it was a REAL baseball family. It was really great when my Daddy got his nice Magnavox radio—we could really hear clearly. These days you turn on the radio and Harry Caray is not on and it's just not like listening to baseball anymore.

St. Louis is just a big, little town...everybody seems to know someone else and we're all connected in some way. That's why the sports figures all like staying here because they never fall into obscurity here, they're always so special. There's always going to be someone to remember them. And, you know, they are so good with the charities as well.

—**Sue Tretter**, Maryland Heights, MO

In 1983, we went to see the Pittsburgh Pirates at Busch Stadium. My dad was supposed to pick us up in the ninth inning. The game went seventeen innings. When we came out after the seventeenth inning, I thought I was going to be in so much trouble, but Dad was still sitting there. He wasn't mad; he was actually excited because he had listened to the whole game! It was a good father-son moment. I wasn't worried that he wouldn't still be out there waiting, I was just worried that he was going to be mad for having to sit out there for so long. He wasn't. What a great dad!

—**Michael Breeding**, St. Louis, Missouri

*The New York Yankees, Brooklyn Dodgers and New York (baseball) Giants banned **RADIO** coverage of their regular-season games between 1934 and 1938...fearing damage to their attendance.

My first memory of Cardinals baseball was when I was six years old, with my grandfather. He lived in the boot heel of Missouri. We would go down there in the summer time and it really didn't matter what time dinner was as long as it was finished by 7:00 P.M. so that we could go out onto the big front porch and turn to **KMOX*** on the transistor radio and just listen to the Cardinals game. It didn't matter where or who they were playing; if it was on the West Coast, that just meant that we would be up late. That was one of the benefits of going to Grandma and Grandpa's—you knew that you would get to listen to the entire game no matter what time it was. That was Grandpa's passion and he instilled it in me. Those are my fondest memories of my grandfather...sitting on that front porch listening to the Cardinal games.

I grew up with Jack Buck and Mike Shannon broadcasting the games. I listened all through high school, college and beyond. I got a job in Chicago and on clear nights I was able to pick up KMOX so that I could listen to the Cardinal games and not have to be forced to deal with the Cubs. That's what was instilled in me; if you're from St. Louis, you listened to the Cardinals game on the radio. It was much more enjoyable listening on the radio than watching them on TV because you could see the game as you wanted to see it but through other people's eyes. You hear the stories. You hear how the announcers were creative in the way they tell the stories.

My favorite players were more the fan favorites, not the superstars—Rex Hudler and Brian Jordan. They would just absolutely go all out, not caring if they were the star or not. They just hustled and put in the hard work...the Cardinal Way. Rex Hudler was, by far, my favorite. To this day, the only fan letter that I've ever written to somebody was to him. I got back a nice autographed glossy from him! He was the epitome of not

---

***KMOX**'s first broadcast of a Cardinals game occurred during the 1926 World Series, and starting in 1927, they began broadcasting the regular season games also.

caring if he was the star or not. He was just going to play the Cardinal Way. He would hustle and give everything. The man would carry multiple gloves depending on where they needed him for a given game.

It was the summer of '86. The Cardinals had a rain-out earlier in the year against the Dodgers. The Dodgers were back in mid -summer. It was their last trip in town so they had to get the games in. They were scheduled for a twilight double-header on a Tuesday with a 5:30 P.M. start and the second game immediately following. They never do that anymore. A buddy of mine came in at noon for lunch. I said, "Hey, what are you doing tonight?" He said, "Nothing." That was back in the days when you could go down and get bleacher tickets on the day of the game so I said, "Let's go down to the Cardinal game?" He said, "Okay."

We got down to the game around 5:30 and there's a rain delay. The first game of the doubleheader ended up starting about 7:45 P.M. and got done about 11 P.M. They start the second game and we moved from the bleachers down to the third row behind home plate because everyone had gone home. We got out of there at 2:00 A.M., the Cardinals swept the double-header! We went back to work the next morning and he came in for lunch and says, "Hey, what are you doing tonight?" I said, "NO WAY!" The Cardinals had a second doubleheader sched-uled—back to back doubleheaders. He said, "Oh, we've got to!" That was the extent of the conversation! "Okay!! We're going!!"

So we went back down to the Stadium to buy tickets for the Cardinal's doubleheader! They won the first game and they won the second game which was the fourth game of the series. They won 4 games in 25 hours! It was amazing! That was back in the day when they didn't care about the gate, they had to get the games in. It was a blast!

—**John Bell**, City of Bridgeton Athletic Director, Bridgeton, MO

In 1956 Red Schoendienst bought the bowling alley three houses away from us. I was only 11 years old. When we heard he bought it, we had to go visit. Red, Ken Boyer, Stan Musial and Don Blasingame would take us out to the back of the bowling alley where there was a little ball field and they would hit us pop flies! When Red would hit a pop fly, we would stand right up under it. First it would almost go out of sight, and then when you could see it coming down to you, you'd think, "Ok I've got it!" The next thing you know, it would land about 10-12 paces to the left or right of you...every time! It was funny!

—**Jerry Bradshaw**, Herculaneum, MO

My experience with baseball was the sandlot games played with other kids in the neighborhood. My cousins were avid Cardinal fans and were always bragging about the games they'd go see. My parents could never afford to let me go with my cousins to St. Louis, but I could dream. We took turns wearing my cousin Mike's red Cardinal ball cap as we played ball in his back yard. I felt so important while wearing that cap. I hated when my turn was over and I had to take it off. We went to visit my cousins in St. Louis. A cousin that was my age of nine showed me his pennants, t-shirts, hats and baseball cards he had collected over the years. He told me stories of Bob Gibson and Steve Carlton. He was only nine but he had a lot of Cardinal baseball items and Cardinal knowledge. I fell in love with the logo of the two cardinals sitting on the bat. He told me about a kids club I could join. He gave me the address of the club at Busch Stadium and he told me to write. As soon as I got home I wrote and, boy, was I surprised a few weeks later when a packet arrived at my doorstep. Inside was a team picture of the Cardinals, a membership card, some Cardinal stickers and a few rookie cards. How I treasured those items! They finally got lost in one of our many moves but I was hooked! I told my wife that I have three wishes before I die. One day, I'd like to be able to afford season tickets to the Cardinals at Busch Stadium in the bleacher section, I would like to own a jukebox and third, a Coca-Cola vending machine. Hey, one can dream, can't they?

—**Robert Jaeckel**, Cardinal fan since 1964

I have memories of the hundreds of nights my dad and I sat quietly listening to Harry and Jack and Joe Garagiola, no lights on in the house, just the sound of the Cardinals. My grandmother gave me Cardinal stuff and talked baseball with me often. In the early '50s, the Cardinals were struggling defensively with the infield. Ray Jablonski and Alex Grammas were the third baseman and shortstop. My grandmother wrote Harray Caray a letter suggesting that the team buy some red aprons for the infielders to wear, thus stopping all those ground balls from going between their legs. Harry was so amused that he read it on the air. We were living in Lawrenceburg, Tennessee, at the time and my grandmother was in Bristow, Oklahoma. My dad was sure that his mom was the one who wrote the letter. He wrote her and asked if she had written it, and she said that she had. We laughed at her sense of humor often, but that was one of her best moments.

—**Carl Taylor**, Russell, Kentucky; Cardinal fan since 1952

I remember playing in the front yard at night and listening to Jack Buck and Mike Shannon describe the action at Busch Stadium or riding home in the car after **LITTLE LEAGUE*** games and listening to Buck or Shannon call a game from Dodger Stadium or Candlestick Park. Even though the Cardinals were not the best in the National League at the time, I became a huge fan of Al Hrabosky, Ted Simmons, Garry Templeton, Ken Reitz and Bake McBride, who Mike Shannon called the Callaway Kid because he was from nearby Fulton, Missouri. When I was nine, my father took a position with the Missouri Automobile Dealers' Association and traveled to St. Louis once a month for business. He usually stayed at the Chase Park Plaza Hotel and sometimes visited a tavern nearby called Nick's Place. My father met Al Hrabosky there one night and over a period of time, Al

*Starting in 1997, the number of participants in **LITTLE LEAGUE**
Baseball has declined by half a million youngsters…from 2.6 million to 2.1 million.

and my father became friends. Al introduced my father to other Cardinals such as Ted Simmons—who is still my favorite Cardinal—and Garry Templeton to name a few.

As my father tells it, Al was about as colorful off the field as he was on. He would always say, "Psych Up!" and that is the way he autographed balls, caps and pictures which we still have from him. My father remembers when Vern Rapp told Al to shave off the Fu Man Chu mustache. Al said something like, "How can I intimidate hitters if I look like a golf pro?" During the 1977 season Al invited my father and me down to the dugout prior to a Cubs-Cardinals game. I still have the scorecard—35 years later. We received a VIP pass to allow us to go into the dugout and visit with Al. It was really neat to be with the entire team and meet such a popular ballplayer. Al gave me a baseball signed by the whole team which fulfilled a childhood fantasy for me. Unfortunately, he was traded to Kansas City and my father eventually lost touch with him. It is great now to watch Cardinal baseball games from Arkansas and see Al back in the Cardinal family. So many Cardinals seem to come back to St. Louis and I think those of us who grew up in that environment know why it is such a special team and a special place—unlike Cub fans.

—**Shawn Jungmeyer**, Fayetteville, Arkansas

My earliest memories are listening to Jack Buck and Harry Caray broadcasting Cardinal games during the 1950s. In 1963 my sisters were in high school. At the end of the year the school bus driver would take the kids on a trip. That particular year the trip was to St. Louis for a day at the Highlands and a baseball game at Sportsman's Park against the **MILWAUKEE BRAVES***. Somehow, I managed to be included in the trip even though I was only 12 years old at the time. We got to St. Louis and stopped at the Steak 'n Shake at Germania and Gravois for a

*The **MILWAUKEE BRAVES** (1953–1965) were the only major league team never to have a losing season.

sandwich. The manager of the restaurant told us we had to park the bus across the street in the parking lot of a bowling alley. We were all sitting there on our bus in the bowling alley parking lot eating our sandwiches when a red Corvette pulled up. The driver got out and asked us what we were doing parked there. We explained the situation and told him our plans for the day. He said, "Wait right here." The driver went inside the bowling alley—called Redbird Lanes—and came out with a stack of publicity photos and signed one for every kid that was on the bus. He signed, "#6, Stan Musial". What a great ambassador for the Cardinals and the game of baseball.

I now live in Champaign, Illinois and the rivalry here is intense between the Cub and Cardinal fans. When people ask me whether I'm a Cub fan or a Cardinal fan, my favorite response is, "I hate the **CUBS***. I hate their wives. I hate their kids and I hate their dogs." Then I ask them if they are a Cub fan. If they say, "Yes", I tell them, "That's fine. I will talk slower." I love asking Cub fans if they know that Missouri named a portion of Interstate 70 in honor of McGwire. When most of them tell me that they knew that, I ask them if they knew Chicago named a street after Sosa. When they don't know, I tell them, "Yes, Second Street."

—**Larry Martin**, area sales manager for Collegiate Apparel, Champaign, IL

*Steve Goodman wrote the song "Go, Cubs, Go" played after every home **CUB** victory. He also wrote "A Dying Cub Fan's Last Request," "Do They Still Sing The Blues When Opening Day Rolls Around In Chicago?", "The City of New Orleans" and "You Never Even Called Me By My Name," a hit song for David Allan Coe. Goodman was to sing the National Anthem before Game 1 of the 1984 NLCS at Wrigley but he died twelve days earlier. He was replaced by his friend Jimmy Buffett.

Chapter Two

BUSCH STADIUM

Home Sweet Home St. Louis

BINGO, I MUST BE IN THE FRONT ROW

JIM CLAUSER

Jim Clauser, origi-nally from the small town of Pawnee, Illinois, has been a season ticket holder in the bleachers since 2003. Clauser and a crew of 150 friends and family attended 14 consecutive Opening Days. Clauser works as a financial analyst in Hazelwood, Missouri, and lives with his family in Florissant, Missouri.

Back in 2009, when the All-Star Game came to Busch Stadium, we had the option to purchase tickets for all of the various All-Star events. They were pretty pricey! My wife was a little worried about the money we were spending and she wasn't sure if she wanted to go to all of the activities like the Home Run Derby, the **ALL-STAR GAME*** and the other functions during the All-Star festivities. A good friend of mine is really into baseball and was wanting to go to the Home Run Derby. My wife, being the cool lady that she is, decided she would forgo the Home Run Derby so that I could take my buddy with me.

That was back on July 13, 2009. It was really hot that day. We got down there super early. The gates opened up at 3 o'clock in the afternoon and we got there around 1:30 to wait in line so that we could be one of the first ones through the gate. We wanted

Carlos Beltran is the only player since 1997 to play the full nine innings in an **ALL-STAR GAME...The last write-in player to make the All-Star starting lineup was Steve Garvey in 1974.*

to make sure we were the first ones there to get lots of pictures down close; to get pictures of the guys taking batting practice and working out before the Home Run Derby. We waited for an hour and a half until the gates opened. We got through the gates and we walked directly down on the third base side to get right up close. Our goal was to be the first people down there.

The National League took batting practice and when they were wrapping it up, the American League came out on the field. The usher came down and announced that there were 10 minutes left before we would have to leave that area. They wanted to make sure everybody was able to get in their seats in time for the event. Well, my buddy and I wanted to get pictures of the American League players, so he just said, "Hey, look for an open seat and sit down—the first seat you see! Let's just sit down until the guys are getting out of here. That will buy us a little time and then we can get up and take more pictures." We walked up to the first open seats that we saw about six rows back so they were real close. We sat down right at the end of the aisle. The usher looked at us. I think she knew that we weren't supposed to be there. Then my buddy, with his quick thinking, says, "Hey! Would you take a picture of us?" and he handed the usher our camera. It kind of threw her off! "Yeah...yeah... I'll take your picture." That preoccupied her a bit. She took our picture and we thanked her. The picture turned out great, by the way! She forgot about us after that and went on her way.

We were no more than six rows back, just a little past the third base line. Our normal seats—the seats that we were supposed to be in were up in left field, section 434—two rows from the top. They were way up top! While we were just sitting there, time rolled on and on. The other seats started to fill up. We were expecting to get bumped but as it was getting closer and closer to the actual Home Run Derby, no one had come. Seven o'clock rolls around and the event starts. Literally, all the seats were full! Everybody's there...they're all FULL...and we thought, "Well, maybe these people are running late." We're sitting there and nobody showed up all night long! We saw on the ticket stubs from the guy sitting behind us that the tickets would have cost us $550 each! They were ridiculously expensive and we sat there the whole time. My tickets for way up in section 434 were $135 a seat for the Home Run Derby and $160 each for the All-Star Game.

Jim Clauser (right) and friend in their newly discovered seats

We couldn't even get up to go to the restroom, we were just stuck down there because the ushers were checking tickets so it was hard to get back into that section. We knew that once we left, we would never came back without a ticket stub. Later, we made friends with the people around us and they let us use their ticket stubs to go back and forth to the restroom when we had to.

It was absolutely amazing! We had a great night! My friend was so excited…we were so ecstatic! We couldn't believe what was happening. It was so unbelievable…a once-in-a-lifetime opportunity…literally, those were the only seats that nobody showed up for.

Fast-forward to the next day. My wife came with me to the All-Star Game and my buddy who was with me the night before, was trying to get a ticket one way or another to go to the All-Star Game. I took my wife early. I said, "Hey...just for fun, we should walk down to those seats that we sat in last night...since nobody showed up for the Home Run Derby...I guess there's a chance maybe, that no one will show up for the All-Star Game either." She said, "Yeah, do you know what fat chance means?" We went down and sat in the seats. We saw the same guys that were sitting behind us and all around us the night before and we were talking to them. They were laughing about the night before saying, "Man we can't believe you got to sit down here... just unbelievable!"

Well, the same thing happened that night! Nobody showed up the entire **ALL-STAR GAME***! I literally think these were the only two seats that were not taken in the entire Stadium, and we just happened to pick those out of the blue and sat there!

My buddy from the night before did get into the game. He ended up getting a ticket, it was up in section 350. He called me to let me know he was at the game and said, "Hey, where are you guys at?" I told him, "Man, you are not going to believe it...we're sitting in the same seats that you and I were in last night!" He just about lost it! He couldn't believe it.

As for my wife, she had a really great time. She was just so excited to be there but was apprehensive at first about sitting in those seats. She didn't want to sit down and get bumped. She gets embarrassed when those sort of things happen, but she was definitely excited that we got to sit down there and watch the entire All-Star Game from those seats. That was an unbelievable, once-in-a-lifetime, complete fluke, but man, were those some great memories! I have no idea what ever

*In June of 1945, theatrical producer Mike Todd—then with the USO in France—tried to set up a major league **ALL-STAR GAME** in Nuremburg Stadium. The stadium had a capacity of 120,000 and Todd wanted American GIs to be able to see major league baseball.

happened to the people who really had those seats. The only thing that I can imagine is that maybe they got arrested for trying to scalp tickets...

It is tradition for a lot of the Cardinal players over the years to save up hats, sweatbands and batting gloves...things like that. After the last home game of the season, the players take out all of the stuff they saved up, and just throw it up into the crowd over their dugout. I always start to make my way over to the Cardinals'dugout around the eighth inning because a lot of people know about it; everybody's starting to make their way over there. If you don't have tickets in that section, you have to try to sneak past the ushers and get positioned so right when the game ends you can bum-rush the dugout. That day, I started to make my way over to get my spot, but as usual, everybody started to rush down. I wasn't as quick as I used to be, so I didn't get up close to the dugout. I was about three people back. I was a little too far back and had no chance of getting anything. Right as I was thinking that I was wasting my time, all of a sudden, I see a batting glove! So Taguchi launched his batting glove up in the air and it just floated. "Oh, my gosh...I might have a chance for this thing!" As it gets a little bit closer, I took a jump in the air and pulled it down with one hand. A couple of us were going for the glove, but I came down out of the scrum with it. I was pretty excited! I had consumed a couple of beers, so I was pretty excited to catch anything. Taguchi had signed it in English and also in Japanese. It's pretty cool—a pretty neat souvenir. As I was walking away, the guy that was trying to grab it with me said, "Hey Buddy, I'll give you 75 bucks for that glove right now." I said, "No, no, man—I'm good. It's a pretty cool souvenir, I'm going to hold onto it." He said, "Okay...I just really like Taguchi."

Then, I'm standing there talking to a couple of friends, showing off my glove. That same guy came walking up the aisle. He said,"Hey! I'll give you 125 bucks for it right now. I'll give you 125!" I'm told him again, "No...No...I'm gonna keep it man...I appreciate it, but I really like Taguchi as well and I'm going to hold on to it."

To this day, I have all kinds of baseball memorabilia, and that glove sits there right in the the middle of everything. It's a pretty cool piece, but every time I look at it I think about not taking that 125 bucks...

One of my fondest memories is because my friend, Derek was involved. It was my fondest, but it sucked so bad. In 2004, when the Red Sox beat the Cardinals in the World Series, I was just devastated. I was distraught. We hung around to watch the celebration. My wife and everyone else had already left to go home, but Derek and I stayed down there for a while to take in the history because the Red Sox had not won the World Championship since 1918. If we could have wished for one team to win it, at least it was the Red Sox, because now the Cubs are the only ones that are cursed. The experience was really cool!

The players were all going crazy. **MANNY RAMIREZ*** was absolutely going nuts. Actor Jimmy Fallon ran around on the field with Drew Barrymore too. We had no idea what in the heck they were doing. I found out later that they were filming the end of their movie, *Fever Pitch*. We made our way down behind home plate. The Red Sox players were celebrating with the tons of Boston fans that made it into town for that game. There were probably almost as many Red Sox fans as there were Cardinal fans...there were a lot of them there!

We were just off the third base side of home plate. I had given someone on the field a cup, and he scooped up a bunch of home plate dirt into the cup. I still have that sitting in my house. My most memorable moment from that night was that they had a news crew from Boston doing a live remote from there. I had my

***MANNY RAMIREZ** grew up in the Washington Heights area of New York. His two sons are both named Manny Ramirez, Jr. Vin Scully also grew up in Washington Heights.

blue Cardinal hat on backwards. I was in the front row, right against the wall leaning over the rail next to home plate. They're interviewing Red Sox fans asking them, "How do you feel? What do you think?" All the fans are going crazy—they're going wild and are so excited. Then the TV reporter looked at me and said, "What about you? How do you feel?" I just looked up and turned my hat around so they could see the "STL" on my hat. I had my Cardinal pullover on, but all they could see was red because I had my arms crossed in front of me and my hat was backward. I said, "Obviously, I think it SUCKS!" and they quickly panned away from me and went onto the next guy. I remember all of the Red Sox fans booing. The crew had thought that I was a Boston fan the whole time. Well, at least I got my 2 cents worth in to all of those **BOSTON*** fans back in Beantown.

*The **RED SOX** currently are on the longest string of sell-outs in the history of baseball.

IT WAS A BALL

CRAIG BALL

Craig Ball takes great pride that the game of baseball was passed down to him by his grandfather and his uncles. Nicknamed "Ballgame" by his peers, he is accused of being more than a fan. If you have ever visited the Foot Locker in South County Mall in the last eight years, there is a good chance he engaged you in baseball conversation and you ended up walking out with a new pair of shoes.

Camera Day was always fun. There were always giveaways like Bat Day and Helmet Day, but Camera Day gave you a chance to get up close and see the players. Going on the field was a big deal because they would not let you go on the field for anything else.

They would put barricades up and the players would walk along the barricades and you could snap pictures of them. It was interesting because you would see the players without their hats or helmets on. You never really knew what they looked like without their hats or helmets because most of them kept them on during the games. It was harder to see in the dugouts back then too, because the dugouts were smaller and it was hard see into the open dugout.

It's always been neat over the years looking back at pictures from Camera Day because you could actually see the players standing still. Nowadays, cameras are so fancy you can zoom in and get real close to them. Back then, everything seemed really far away so the only chance of you getting a good shot of a player up close was on Camera Day. It looked more like a baseball card.

Albert Pujols frequently would let kids come underneath the barricade and stand next to him for a picture. Many times, the star players would zip by you real fast and you might be lucky to get a shot of their head or the back of their jersey. But Albert was very good at coming over and shaking hands—especially with young kids.

In 2005 there were a lot of events to commemorate the history of the Stadium. There was a countdown on the outfield wall starting with 81 games and counting down to the last game. If a player matched the number on the wall, they would honor that player on the field. Fredbird would pick them up in his little Fredbird car and drive them around the warning track. It was funny to see Ozzie Smith or Joe Torre or Keith Hernandez riding around with Fredbird in his Fredbirdmobile. A memorable one was the night that Albert tore off #5. If you remember, the old right field wagon gate was a big gate. There was always an issue with the wagon gate—it was just so big and bulky—almost like a large garage door. The gate was cracked open and when I looked down I could see Albert's wife, Deidre, and his two kids walk out onto the warning track just waiting. The kids were facing toward the infield! As Albert was running out to right field from the dugout, you could hear his kids yelling, "Daddy! Daddy! Daddy!" They were jumping up and down as he's approaching. When he got there, he stopped, bent down and his two kids gave him the biggest hug. His kids were just so excited to see him even though they had just seen him a couple hours before. As he peels the "5" off, he hands it to his son. His son stands up on his toes and takes the number 5 from him. It was so neat seeing it up close like that. I knew in 2005 that this moment would be more special as years go by. That's what baseball does—it creates special memories.

Albert Pujols and children, 2005

When we moved into the new Stadium in 2006, it was clean and it was nice! It had that old look to it with the black wrought iron fencing and gates, and the brick—it's a beautiful place but all the memories were still in the old park. If we were going to like this new Stadium, it was going to have to generate some new memories—to win the World Series in its inaugural season was a heck of a start! I missed Jack Buck's voice not being the narrator, but the World Series was spectacular!

I am not sure how many fans noticed but as soon as Wainwright threw the final pitch in that '06 Series, and right before the fireworks exploded, someone played "Go Crazy Folks" over the speaker system.

In 2001, I worked over at the Marriott across from old Busch Stadium at the outside bar. During Albert Pujols' rookie season, on Mother's Day, the game was at an odd time. It wasn't a 1:10 or 7:10 game, it was a goofy time. Having gone to many games and hanging out at the Stadium looking for autographs, I knew players typically got to the park at certain times. You could go down a few hours before game time and could see a lot of the players walking into the Stadium. You could try to get an autograph or just say "Hi" or shake their hands.

That day I was setting up the patio at the hotel bar outside across from the Stadium at the Marriott (now the Hilton). The bar faced the Plaza of Champions—where the big Stan Musial statue was. There were also nine pillars with a flag that represented each of the world championship seasons. It was where most people met before games. On that Mother's Day, I saw Albert Pujols walking down the sidewalk as I was setting up. I cut over to the stairs on the far right hoping he would turn the corner and walk down the sidewalk just so I could say hello or shake his hand. That was common—seeing players cut through the hotel. Every once in a while I'd be able to strike up a conversation with one of them. Unfortunately, Albert didn't come my way, but I saw him cross the street walking by the Plaza of Champions. When he did, he slowed down and looked at them—he paused and stood there a minute in admiration. He then headed down the sidewalk towards the glass doors that lead to the locker room. It was very cool. I had seen many players walk by those statues in the Plaza of Champions, not giving it a second glance. They wouldn't know what the flags were, who the statues were or what it was all about. So seeing Albert look at them and acknowledge the history of Cardinal baseball was just a sign of what was to come. Even though he's not with the Cardinals anymore, you could always tell there was an appreciation, admiration and respect not only for the game and the history but Musial in particular. He was a very special player....

The year 2000 was when I started as a bartender at the Marriott. On my break, I would walk over to Busch for a couple of innings until the bar started getting busy toward the end of the game. Occasionally, customers at the bar would just hand me tickets. There were only two games that entire season I didn't work and I had tickets for both. One night during a **PIRATES*** game, I brought my baseball glove with me and a 7-year-old friend of the family. There were a group of guys sitting near us and they were all laughing at us because we had our gloves. They were drinking beer, joking around, and making stupid, immature comments. It never got into a situation that was a problem. Kevin Young, the first basemen for the Pirates hit a long ball and I leaned over the walkway in section 284. I caught the ball back-handed, down inside the walkway. No one else could reach it because they didn't have a glove. As soon as I caught it, these guys started ribbing each other! One of their buddies was screamin', "He had a glove, you didn't! He had a glove, you didn't!"

I gave the ball to the boy I was with. Someone at the end of the aisle started yelling, "Throw it back!" Next thing you know, everyone around us was saying "Throw it back!" The little boy is not throwing it back. This guy kept going on for a half of an inning. I was getting ticked off and walked down to where they were sitting. "Is there something you want to say?" People got in between us and said, "Hey, hey! It's okay." The usher came down to see what was going on, and I said, "This guy is using foul language. I have a kid with me, and I don't appreciate it.

*From 1933 to 1939, the NFL's Pittsburgh Steelers were named the Pittsburgh **PIRATES**. The Pittsburgh Pirates was also the name of a National Hockey League team in the 1920's...In September 2010, Pittsburgh Penguins star Sidney Crosby took batting practice with the Pirates and hit a 370-foot "home run" that almost cleared the Park.

He wants us to throw the ball back." They talked to the guy and it got resolved...no big deal. I sat back down and started talking to the guys that were razzing me. I said, "That will never happen to me again! I will never be in a position where I could possibly get in a fight over something so stupid"...

The very next game, we were sitting out in the Batter's Eye Club in dead centerfield. Tickets there included food and drink on the inside, but your seat was outside. This was July 4th and it was hotter than a two dollar hooker on a submarine. We're 12 rows up and six seats in from the aisle. My brother-in-law was a police officer in town from Jacksonville, Illinois and he had to leave around the 6th inning. We rarely sat in the outfield, but when you do sit out there, you think you have a chance for a ball. So I brought my glove again, but I also brought a spare baseball in the event I would catch one...I wouldn't have to throw the home run ball back. It's the 6th inning and my brother-in-law said that he had to get going to get back to get to his shift in time. I said, "Alright! I'll save the home run ball for you!" He just laughed and left.

An inning later, Michael Tucker from the Cincinnati Reds hits a deep drive into centerfield. It's 100 degrees, and we're staring right into the sun. The ball was hit hard. The crowd made it sound like it was coming to the bleachers, but I couldn't see it. I knew it was hit hard enough, so I looked at Jim Edmonds on the field as he was running back hard toward the wall. I jumped over the people sitting next to me and ran down the steps. As I'm running down the steps, I was watching Edmonds running to the wall. I just made a straight line with Edmonds. When I ran out of steps and got down to the front row, I leaned over, looked up and the ball was right over the grass in that little center field area and it landed right in my glove...backhanded.

I almost wanted to give it to Edmonds and say, "Here! Maybe they won't notice I caught it!" Edmonds looked right at me, and he starts walking back to his position. Everyone was patting me on the back. A couple of people were saying, "Hey!

We'll buy you a beer!" Then I heard the chant, "Throw it back! Throw it back!" I look around and I'm considering throwing it back. The usher comes down and says, "Hey! You made a great catch! I have to get your name and address because the Cardinals are going to send you something." I asked, "Am I going to get in trouble if I throw it back?" She said, "No. No. No. You don't have to throw it back." I clarified. "I'm asking you if I will get in trouble if I throw it back. Are you going to kick me out?" She said, "No. I'm not going to kick you out." I reach into my bag and grab this other baseball, stand up and throw it as far as I can. It hopped twice and rolled to Renteria at shortstop. He turned around, caught it and flipped it toward the **REDS*** dugout for Tucker to keep as a souvenir. When I got back to my seat, there were people offering to buy me beer for throwing it back. Well, I was in the Batter's Eye Club so beers and food were free for us. I was handed a beer and I gave it to someone else since I already had one. I was sitting there looking at this ball and this girl said, "You didn't have to do that!" I said, "Well...I didn't." She asked, "What do you mean, you didn't?" I showed her the ball, and because it was the 4th of July, MLB had a special Stars and Stripes logo on the home run ball.

The next half inning, as Michael Tucker comes out to take his position in center field, he looks up at me with a smile and mouths, "Yeah. Right." He knew I tossed a dirty 'ole ball back in to them. My intention was to get the ball signed at some point. It's still unsigned. Part of that story is that on my birthday, a couple years later, my wife, bought me a print from the Marquess Gallery called, "Caught Again". It was a glove with a baseball in it, so I have those two balls that I caught upon a shelf with the "Caught Again" print...

*In 1998 the Cincinnati **REDS** started an outfield trio of Chris Stynes, Dimitri Young, and Mike Frank. You might know them better as Young, Frank, and Stynes. (The author couldn't resist. He'll show himself to the principal's office now.)

At the old Stadium, when Jack Buck passed away, we placed one of my caps on his statue. We wrote on the bill on the cap, "We'll miss you, JFB" and put the hat on his statue head. We decided that after each future World Series victory...every home game we won during the World Series...we would put a new hat on the statue. Come 2004, we thought we were going to get to put hats on Jack, but we got swept by Boston. In '06, each night the Cardinals won a game, we would write a little note on a hat and put it on the statue. "Hey Jack, we're going crazy again!" We would only do it for home games, not the away games.

After Game 1 of the 2006 World Series, my daughter and I walked outside the Stadium but my wife wanted to go home. I said, "Wait! We have to do one more thing!" I handed her the camera as we walked toward the statue. There was a police officer by the statue. We thought maybe he was guarding it to prevent anyone from doing something out of the ordinary, but it turns out he was just watching the street. We walk up and write on a hat, "That's a winner—Game 1". My daughter was sitting on my shoulders and reaches over to put the hat on Jack Buck. We talked to the police officer for a bit, and noticed how many people stopped to take a picture of the statue with the hat on Jack's head!

Come Games 6 and 7, we didn't have the money to get tickets—prices skyrocketed! We ended up tailgating with some friends out on the parking lot. After Game 6, we put a hat on the statue and went out tailgating for a long time. We could see the statue in the distance. We kept checking to see how long the hat would stay on his head because people kept trying to take the hat. When they tried, someone standing there taking pictures or just looking at it would pressure the person trying to steal it to put it back. It became a game to see how long the hat would last on there. I went over to it a couple of times and saw about 30 people getting their pictures taken with it. I actually have a video of someone trying to take the hat. I walked up to the guy and said, "Hey! Is that your hat?" He just looked at me and I said, "You need to put that back on Mr. Buck." He just looked at me again and I said, "Flip it over. I bet there is a #8 written on the inside bill of the hat." He flipped it over and sure enough, there was a #8. He laughed and said, "No disrespect man!" and he put it back on the statue.

This went on for a period of time...an hour and a half after the game. Out of the blue, this guy (see photo at left) walked up to our tailgate, and he is wearing the hat! We didn't see him take the hat! We asked, "Where did you get that hat?" He said, "This is my hat!" I replied, "You took that hat from Mr. Buck!" He just looked at me and we looked over to the statue and the hat was still on it! We couldn't figure out how he got it off because it was definitely the same one. He said, "I didn't take any hat." I said, "I'll bet you, under that hat, there is a name and number and it's the same one that's underneath my jacket." I turned around and dropped down my jacket and showed him the name and number on the back of my jersey. He said, "I didn't mean any disrespect! I didn't take it, I traded it! I'm just trying to have a good time. I love the Cardinals! Look at me! I'm dressed in full uniform!" I said, "Well, you need to take that back over there." He starts shaking my hand and apologizing. We took a picture of him standing by our barbecue grill in the parking lot and then watched him walk over and switch the hats. He came back over and drank a beer with us and talked baseball...

At old Busch Stadium, they had an event called "Blast Out of Busch". When the Cardinals were on the road, they would have a day for this event. Regular people were given a chance to go to the Stadium and try to hit a home run. Everyone thinks it's so easy to go out on the field and jack one out. Well, with "Blast Out of Busch", you could pay a certain price, and they would give you five pitches. All money went to charity. They had batting practice pitchers on the field with batting cages. You would get in there and take your cuts. You could bring your own bat.

If you hit a home run you would get a little plaque that said "I blasted one out of Busch Stadium" and an autographed ball from the team. People thought they would be giving away tons of baseballs. I went down there with the thought I was going to jack one out of Busch. Well, I didn't jack one out of Busch, I bounced two off the wall—one in right center field and one in left center field. I felt pretty good. The following season, they were going to do it again, and the prizes were a little better because not many people had done it the year before. I'm thinking, "I'm getting one out of there this year!" My buddy calls a bunch of friends of mine to come down to Busch.

I went down during my designated time, and I'm confident! I know I'm hitting one out! I'm thinking of which way I wanted to go...opposite field or pull one down the line?

I'm one of the few left-handers in line. They had several hundred that had already finished. I noticed while I'm waiting my turn that the pitcher was bringing it pretty good; worse, he was left-handed. I didn't like batting against left-handers. I'm standing on the dugout step, and all my buddies are up in the stands. We all graduated from the same high school, Hazelwood Central. They had all seen me play before so I was comfortable that I was going to hit one out of Busch! The first pitch, the pitcher fires one and it hit about an inch away from my hands on the inside of my bat. It was a foul ball! I had an aluminum bat so my hands were stinging! My buddies were razzing me. Next one was a foul ball again. My hands were ringing from that first pitch. I'm thinking, "I have to get one out of here...I had success last year!" I didn't even get it out of the infield. The year before, with no one in the stands, I was hitting them off the wall. I had to walk back and face these guys. That's the memory I have of" Blast Out of Busch"...all my buddies seeing me hit a worm burner. ...

When Jack Buck passed away, the fans put together a big shrine to his memory. I went down that night, with an American flag, a rose and a Cardinal hat. I sat across the street so I could still see the statue. As I sat there, Chris Benoit of Fox News made his way over to me. He asked me what I thought of Jack Buck. I told him, "This guy is a true patriot. Everything I know about him is incredible. He's the voice of all my memories at this Stadium. Every memory I've ever had, he was there." I told him about being a teenager and walking back with Jack Buck to his car. When I first introduced myself to Jack Buck, I told him that I had collected money for Cystic Fibrosis. He was the chairperson for that foundation. That was my ice-breaker when I went to say "hello" to him. Every night after the game, we would be getting autographs and would end up walking with him to his car. He knew me by name and he would just talk to me about the game. I was 15 years old. I remember the first time he remembered my name. He said, "Hi Craig! What did you think about the game tonight?" We talked about that game. Willie McGee had made a diving catch and hurt his hip. Hearing his voice was like God talking to you. It was the voice to narrate all my memories. Benoit said, "We're going to go live with KMOX pretty soon. Would you mind telling your story again?"

I'll always remember Jack Buck's voice, "Hey Craig! What did you think of the game tonight?" As he was getting into his car, he would say, "See you tomorrow night!" I never thought about that until right now, but he would say that. I have goose bumps now!...

In 2003 at old Busch Stadium, the Cardinals had an open house event for season ticket holders. Usually it was held on a Sunday prior to a Sunday night game to allow people enough time to get in and out of the Stadium before the gates opened for the game. The players would be there and there were all kinds of events and games set up. You could tour the dugout and even the clubhouse. There were players throughout the Stadium signing autographs or posing for pictures. For instance, they would have Scott Rolen up in the Stadium Club out in left field while Albert Pujols would be down in the Red Bird Inn, which was on the lower level down the left field line. And Fernando Vina was out in the "The Birds Nest" in centerfield. They would spread these guys out around the park for an hour at a time.

We wanted to get a picture with Albert Pujols. He wasn't signing autographs, it was just pictures. Rolen was signing autographs up in the Stadium Club. We realized because their times overlapped, that it would be hard to do both. We decided to go down to the Red Bird Inn. We got in line, knowing that we would get cut off before we got to see Jim Edmonds who was there before Albert, but we would still be close to the front of the line for Albert. As soon as we could get through the line to see Albert, we could go upstairs to the Stadium Club where Scott Rolen was, because my wife Beth really wanted to see Scott Rolen.

The Cardinals had an usher walking along Pujols' line saying, "No autographs. You can take your picture or we can have someone take it for you." We were trying to decide how we were going to get this picture of the two of us with Albert? We were concerned that if we had someone else take the picture, we wouldn't know how it was going to turn out. At that time, it was the beginning of the new digital camera age. We had just bought a new digital camera and weren't sure how good it was going to work.

We were in line waiting for Edmonds when the line cut off so then we were in the front of the line for Albert. The person in charge announced, "Only one picture with Albert, so you either both have to be in the picture at the same time or if you want to take it yourself, the other person doesn't get to have a picture with him." I told Beth, "Let's both get in the picture and have someone else take it." She said, "Do you want to risk it getting messed up?" I said, "That's okay, if that's all we can do, then that's all we can do." She said, "You know what...I'll take your picture with Albert and you take a picture of me with Rolen."

Then Beth takes a picture. It was a nice photo. As we're about to walk out of the line, Beth said to Albert, "I just want to shake your hand." He steps over to shake hands with Beth and said, "You don't want a picture?" She looks over at the usher said, "Uh, we're only supposed to have one." He said, "No, it's okay!" He puts his arm around her, they get their picture taken and they're smiling real big. So we each got a picture with Albert. She shook his hand again and said, "Thanks a lot." He smiled and said, "Thank you!" How cool was that for him to reach out to shake hands and then for him to say, "No...let's do the picture."

When the All-Star Game came to St. Louis in 2009. FanFest was a big interactive event held at the America's Center. I went to the Stadium to buy tickets on my way to work. The lady asked me, "Do you want your tickets now or do you want to pick them up from Albert?" I was told that Albert Pujols was going to hand out tickets to the first one hundred people that were buying tickets, but to my amazement there were only thirty people in line. I asked, "Albert is going to be here at the window?" She said, "No. If you go to The Team Store at 2 o'clock, he's going to be there to hand out the tickets. You can take them now or you can come back to get your tickets." I said, "Well, I'll come back in three hours and pick them up from Albert. That would be tremendous!" I starting thinking, "What am I going to do here? I have got to see Albert and my daughter is at the babysitter. I would love for her to be with me when I get the tickets from Albert."

I called up my buddy Mike and told him about it. I told him, "Albert is going to be here handing out the tickets. Your kids can all meet Albert." His kids all play baseball and softball so I knew they would be interested. He said, "No. I don't think they will want to do it because they're at the pool right now."

Then I called up my buddy Jim. I told him about Albert handing out the tickets and asked him if he wanted to come down. He said, "Yeah, I heard about that on the news last night, but you can't get autographs and you can't take pictures." I said, "It doesn't matter. Albert is going to be there handing out the tickets! Your kids will get to meet Albert!" He said, "Yeah, but if they can't get autographs, they are going to be disappointed." I said, "Okay."

Then I called my wife, I said, "Beth, what time does Alivia take her nap?" She said, "She's probably taking it right now." I said, "Albert is going to be here at The Team Store handing out the tickets. I would like to bring her down here to get the tickets from Albert." She said, "Well, go get her then." I said, "You don't care if I go wake her up?" She said, "No. Go get her and take her back down."

She was 20 miles away at the babysitter's.

I tried to get my buddies to bring their kids down and they all turned me down because they couldn't get autographs or take pictures. I thought it was a big deal to me. The All-Star Game had not been here since '66, so it was cool that our star player... the featured guy of the All-Star Game was going to be there.

So I hustled out to St. Charles to pick her up from the babysitter's. Then I hustled back home to get her little baseball cap and hustled back down there. Now anybody that you know that has a baby, especially a man...it's a lot more challenging to get a baby from point A to point B. Getting the stroller ready... getting the diaper bag ready...getting all of these things that you need whenever you're out and about with a baby. I didn't like to venture off too far from home without my wife the baby expert.

Parking around the Stadium was horrible. I had to park three blocks away. The whole process of getting her in and out of the car was like a scene from a Chris Farley movie. I'm sweating, bumping into things and dropping stuff. I started hustling down the sidewalk because it was getting close to the time that he was going to be there and the Cardinals never said how long he was going to stay.

After huffing and puffing down the sidewalk we get to the entrance of The Team Store. I see Albert but there is nobody in line. There were just some people behind a roped off area just standing around looking at him. Almost everybody had already been through the line so we were the last ones. There were two envelopes sitting on the table. Rene Knott, the sportscaster from Channel 5 was there at the front of the roped area where we had to enter.

The fact that she was only one and a half might seem that she was too small or she may not remember. I thought it was a pretty big deal and wanted her to be there. What if she grows up loving baseball, she'll be able to tell her friends her daddy took her to the last one at Busch decades before.

Albert is standing there with the envelope in his hand. He handed it to my daughter, but she curled up towards my shoulder, so I took the envelope. I told her, "Say 'Hi' to Albert!" She was clinching really tight onto my shoulder. There were news cameras everywhere. There were many media people crowded around along with many fans who were there to shop and just see Albert up close. She was a little freaked out by the crowd.

We were standing there and I shook his hand. He had won the "Roberto Clemente Award" the year before so I said, "Congratulations on the Clemente Award. Not only is it one of my favorite awards I think it is one of the best in baseball." I had a yellow All-Star Jersey from the 2006 game in Pittsburgh on with his number "5" on the back. He said, "Thank you" and nodded his head. I said to my daughter, "Say 'Hi' to Albert" but she wouldn't even look at him. After a minute or so, we started to leave the line without her saying anything to him or even looking at him. I heard him say to the guy that was standing there, "I thought that I was good with kids?" I thought, "Oh...I can't leave on that note." So I stopped and turned around and said, "Albert, you gotta give her a second chance, she's a good kid." I said, "Say 'Hi' to Albert...say 'Hi' to Mr. Pujols." She started to raise her head up just a little bit, but she wouldn't turn around. He tickled her on her side, touched her arm and tried to grab her hand but she wasn't responding. I have no idea why I said this...I have never asked her to do this before...but the little girls that live next door to us, Emily and Darby, taught her how to do a fist bump. I said, "Give Albert 'knuckles.'" I don't why I said it? She raised her head up off of my shoulders. She looked both ways at all of the cameras. Albert had put his fist up and held it there for a second. She turned around and looked at him and she bopped his knuckles.

The place just exploded..."Aww!" There were all kinds of photos being taken...all you heard was click,click,click. As soon as she did it, she dove right back into my shoulder. As she rested her head on my shoulder, I just pointed to Albert as we walked out of the line. Just as we got out the line, someone from Fox 2 News came over and said, "Hey you just had a really neat moment with Albert there. Can we talk to you?" I made the comment about how the All-Star Game had not been here since 1966 and the next time the All-Star Game rolls around, my daughter may be there but I probably won't. I got choked up trying to get the words out about me not being there.I was thinking of my grandfather who taught me baseball and my one-and-a-half-year-old daughter who I will teach baseball. I just had to turn my head away from the camera.

When we were about to leave, a lady from the Associated Press came over and said, "Hey, my photographer got pictures… if you want to give me your email, I will try to send them to you." It had said, "No photographs. No autographs."…that was why my buddies didn't want to bring their kids down. I got some information from her and as we started to walk out. I was thinking, "Darn, that was pretty cool!"

It made all three newscasts.

The next day we were out walking early in the morning, through our neighborhood. I was pulling my daughter around in her big red wagon. A lot of our neighbors know that we're Cardinals fans and anytime we're walking around, they wave to us… even though we may not have talked to each other too much. My neighbor Rob peeked his head out and said, "Hey! It's the celebrities!" I smiled and said, "What channel did you see us on? He said, "Oh no..no…The newspaper!" I said, "The newspaper?" He said, "You didn't see it?" I said, "No, I don't know anything about it?" He said, "Well, let me go grab it!" He brings it out and he shows me. It's a black and white picture of Alivia leaning on my shoulder with her head tucked down and Albert has a big smile on his face.

A quick flashback: My grandfather had given me this beautiful red,white and blue bunting from the '66 All-Star Game. He had passed away shortly before she was born. A couple days later, we were at my mom's house for a barbecue. I showed my family the newspaper and they couldn't believe that she was in the newspaper. My three aunts were gathered around, looking at it too. I was telling them about our experience and I noticed that my Mom's eyes are getting misty. I said, "What is wrong? This is kind of cool. It's supposed to be something happy." I looked at my aunts and their eyes are watery too. They just looked at each other and nodded their heads. I asked them, "What's wrong with you guys?" They said, "Look who took the picture." I said, "Look who took the picture?" They pointed down at the bottom of the newspaper and the guy who took the picture had the same name as my grandfather's—John White—who had worked the All-Star Game in '66. That's got to mean something and it was all a pretty neat experience.

My daughter was born on Stan Musial's birthday, November 21, 2007. We had decided to take her to her first game when the Cardinals were re-dedicating Stan's statue in front of the Stadium. When they had the re-dedication ceremony, they brought Stan out on a cart before the game. He was up at home plate for the little ceremony. Musial was classic for always pointing out someone else in the crowd. He got up from his chair, leaned up to the microphone and said, "Do you know why I have a bad knee? Because I hit too many triples!" Of course, the whole place laughed. Immediately after that he said, "Say 'Hi' to my good friend Red Schoendienst over there!" Everybody cheered for Red. Then Stan got back onto the cart.

The giveaway that day was a replica of the Stan Musial statue. A lot of those giveaways are plastic and cheap. Edward Jones was the sponsor for this giveaway. This statue was heavy with a marble-type base and it was really cool.

We went to Winter Warm-Up when my daughter was real little. Whenever I would take her down the hall to the bathroom, we would walk past a room where they had an American bald eagle on display. You could get your picture taken with the eagle, you could listen about the endangered species and about the bird. Fredbird would frequently pop in there too. He would pose for pictures. Every time we walked by the room, my daughter would look in the room and say that she wanted to go in there to see the eagle...however when we tried to walk in there, she got really scared. Instead, we went on down the hall to another seminar. She kept bringing up that she wanted to see the eagle, but every time we would go down there, she didn't want to go in...so we said, "The heck with it..we're not going in there."

Nine months later, out of the blue...she said, "Daddy, I'm not afraid of the eagle anymore." I said, "Okay." She then said, "And I'm not afraid of Fredbird either. I'm going to sing to Fredbird this year." She was only three years old at the time. She was always singing, "Take Me Out To The Ballgame," so we thought, "We'll see what happens"

As the Winter Warm-up grew closer, she was still talking about how she was going to sing to Fredbird. When Fredbird makes an appearance, he is usually in and out quick. It's hard to get him to slow down. You might shake his hand or get a picture with him, or he might "beak" your head. We went to the Winter Warm-up and sure enough, the eagle was there and Fredbird was already in there when we walked past the room. I had to explain to my daughter on the way into the room, "Fredbird may not be able to hear you sing, so you may have to sing loud so that he can hear you." We really didn't think anything would come of it.

We went into the room. There were ten to fifteen people sitting down and there were a couple people having their picture taken. They were all just staring at the eagle and she just started singing to Fredbird. He leaned forward to listen to her and then he put his hand up to tell everybody to be quiet and she just escalated her singing as he was standing there. Everybody was just nodding and Fredbird was nodding as well. When she got to the line, "One, two, three strikes you're out..." Fredbird put his hand up...punching his hand up in the air...or his feather or wing...she did really good and everybody clapped in the room.

We then went into main room where everything was going on and there was a guy named, "Photo Joe." He takes pictures of the people attending the event and he gives them his card. You can buy his pictures through his website from Creve Coeur Camera.

"Photo Joe" was up at the KMOX table talking to somebody. I walked up there to fill out a little sheet to sign up for the drawing they were having for Cardinal season tickets. I filled out the sheet and stuck it in the container. "Photo Joe" said something to me and then I asked him, "What did you think about my daughter's singing?" He had taken some pictures of her and had given me his card. He said, "She did great!" He had told Mark Reardon of KMOX, who was sitting there at the table and was about to go "live" on their remote show coming from the Winter Warm-up. He told Mark, "His little girl just sang, 'Take Me Out To The Ballgame' to Fredbird!" Mark said, "Oh yeah? Was she any good?" Joe nodded his head and said, "She was pretty good!" Mark asked me if she would sing on the air? I told him, "I don't know? She might break into 'Twinkle, Twinkle, Little Star'...I don't know if she would stick to it? If you want, I can go get her, she's over in the kids' room with my wife." He said, "Well, go get her and bring her in here!" I told him, "If you pretend that you are my friend she will probably warm up to you."

They were great with her. She went back behind the table and sat between Mark and Kevin Wheeler, from KMOX. They started talking to her about baseball and asked her who her favorite player was... she told him it was Albert. She told them about her birthday being the same as Stan the Man.. When he went live on the air, he said,"I think that I have met my favorite Cardinal fan in the whole world! Her name is Alivia and she is three and she sang to Fredbird earlier and now she is going to sing a song for us." He started talking to her and she sang the song really great! They all gave her a "high-five" afterwards. She had a really good time with it. That was our first event for that season.

TAKE THIS JOB AND LOVE IT

JAY BRAUN

Jay Braun, a retired school teacher, is living his dream job. For the last 10 years, he has been working as a tour guide at Busch Stadium and as an usher for Cardinal ballgames.

Cardinal baseball started for me when I was five years old—my first game was with my dad at Sportsman's Park. When I was 14, the Cardinals were playing the Dodgers. My favorite pitcher, other than a Cardinal, was **SANDY KOUFAX***, and Sandy Koufax was pitching that day. That's when the bullpens were out by the right field line. He is warming up and I'm down in the first row by the bullpen—I don't have a ticket for that seat, but I'm down there just to get close to him to watch him. I said, "Mr. Koufax, when you're finished warming up, could I have that ball?" He never looked at me. He never answered me. I must have said it 50-100 times. All of a sudden, when his warm-up ended, he looked at me and flipped the ball over, it hit my hands and it fell down. Before I could bend down to get it, another kid swooped down and took it! It was my one opportunity to get a ball from the Hall of Famer, Sandy Koufax. My scouting report probably read, "He was slow, but he had bad hands."

In 1968, I had just gotten married to my wife, Bonnie. We didn't have much money—we were just young kids getting started—

---

*In 1966 **SANDY KOUFAX** won the Cy Young Award and retired. That same year, 12-year-old Ron Howard made more money than Koufax while playing Opie on the "Andy Griffith Show."…When he was a youngster, football coaching legend Woody Hayes was a batboy for the Newcomerstown, OH semi-pro team managed by Cy Young.

but we would go to every game our schedule allowed to see Bob Gibson. He had a remarkable year. His ERA was 1.12 and as a result, baseball lowered the mound, which I talk about all the time in the tours I give at the Stadium. I didn't get to see the '68 World Series because I was up in **JOLIET*** student teaching, but Gibson struck out 17 hitters against Detroit. We have a picture of that in the Cardinal Club—which I also point out in the tour. He was just a remarkable player.

Forty years later, I'm sitting at a batting practice position at the entrance to the Cardinal dugout on Opening Day. It was 2009. In walked Bob Gibson with his Hall of Fame red coat because he is going to throw out an honorary first pitch. I stood up and said, "Mr. Gibson, could I please just shake your hand?" He gave me this funny look like, "Oh…okay." I shook his hand and that was it. He went in the locker room. When he came back out, there was nobody in this foyer so I said, "Can I share this little story with you?" He gave me this look like, "It better be short!" So I shared the story about 1968 when my wife and I did what we could to try to see the games he was pitching in, and what a thrill it was 40 years later to actually be in the same room and shake his hand. He's my idol! He smiled at me and said, "Jay, I think we're going to be friends." What that meant was that whenever he comes in on Opening Day or any other time, he will walk over and we'll shake hands. This past year, we even talked about his knee replacement and about normal stuff! I find him to be just as nice of a gentleman as he was a pitcher…

It was the final game of regular season in 2005. The Cardinals had called together all these former players and had a big ceremony planned for after that final game. At that time, I was an usher working on the lower level of the third base side. After the game

---

* In 1941, the news director at a small radio station in Kalamazoo, Michigan hired Harry Caray who had been employed at a station in **JOLIET**, Illinois. The news director's name was Paul Harvey. Yes, that PAUL HARVEY! "And now, you have the rest of the story…

was over, those of us working on the lower level were asked to go out by the warning track to make sure no fans came onto the field. As part of the ceremony, the Cardinal organization had the Clydesdales come out. They are such a part of Cardinal tradition and special events. So many Opening Days the Clydesdales would prance by you that close, it just gave you the chills! It was no big deal and not for anyone to see, but when they came by me in that final game at old Busch, I saluted. My nephew turns out is an amateur photographer. At our Christmas family gathering, he shows me a photo where he actually captured my salute to the Clydesdales—it was very touching. I had never been that close to them and they are just majestic animals.

Jay Braun salutes the Clydesdales and Gussie's hat.

At the Baseball Writer's Dinner in 2012, one of the greatest people who works at the ballpark was honored...that was Aggie Ceriotti. She really is a neat lady...the perfect person to do the job she's in. She greets all the VIP people and press people coming in. I don't know how she does it—she has great energy. I would love to sit next to her one night and hear all the different things she has to do. She has everyone's cell number in the park that she calls to get things done. She's very good at what she does. If I ever see her while I'm giving a tour, I have to stop and introduce her as the "Queen of Busch Stadium". She'll always talk to the people who are on tour and she really enjoys them. She's like baseball's ultimate receptionist...again, a tribute to the tradition of St. Louis.

She and her husband are extremely close with Whitey Herzog and his wife. At the 2012 dinner, they honored her. She got up and you could tell she was a little nervous in the beginning of her speech. All of a sudden she said, "You know, I'm settling down here and starting to enjoy this!" She was telling a lot of stories and ran a little long but everybody was happy because she had a lot to say. Well, Whitey followed and he said, "Man! I never knew Aggie could talk like that!" He talked about how their families are friends and how they go over and play cards and how she's a great cook. But Whitey said, "I never knew how she could talk! It's like giving whiskey to an Indian!" The crowd just went crazy! That's typical Whitey Herzog! He can make a crowd laugh no matter what he says...

In 1967, I tried to get into a **ARMY RESERVE*** Unit. Eventually I did. It was a special Reserve Unit that was going to go out and do the paperwork for all the Reserve Units throughout the Midwest. In so doing, I met Ted Simmons who was in the same

*The last major leaguer to lose playing time during a season due to **MILITARY SERVICE** was Nolan Ryan of the New York Mets.

unit. There were a lot of pro athletes in that unit—**TIM MCCARVER*** was in that unit too. I remember Cardinal football players but of all the athletes, the one who always did everything just like everybody else was Ted Simmons. He would always do his work in the wintertime. He couldn't go to summer camp with us because he was playing ball. I was always impressed because he didn't want any special treatment.

One game, Bill Madlock slid into second base on a play and took out the Cardinal infielder. The dugouts emptied, it got heated, but no fight though. I went to the game the next day, just in case more was to happen. I saw Ted Simmons bring the lineup card out to home plate. I said to myself, "Something is going to happen!" Simmons brought the card out, and when the Cubs manager came out, they started arguing. Simmons just took his fist and belted him! There was a big brawl at home plate! Simmons was a tough customer. I'm sure his teammates respected him because he was one great player.

The hardest thing to me with Simmons, was going to the '82 World Series and seeing him in a Brewer uniform…it just didn't seem right…

I have been fortunate to give tours in both old Busch Stadium and the new Busch. Back in the old Busch, I was taking a pretty small group of people around and there was a Japanese/American young couple who brought their dad who had come over from Japan to visit them. He was about my age, I would guess, and he could not speak English. We were going through the tour and everything I was saying, they would translate to their dad. When we walked out from behind home plate to get onto the warning track to go over to the Cardinal dugout—the last spot on the tour to take pictures—this gentleman walked over behind home plate and knelt down on his hands and knees.

***TIM MCCARVER** is the only catcher in history to lead the league in triples.

He put his two hands down as if he were in prayer and when he got up, he was crying. His daughter's husband said that in all the years they had seen him, he never showed emotion very much—this was a rare show of emotion. It just impressed upon me the power of baseball. It transcends our political differences. It transcends our religious differences. It even transcends our different cultures. It's amazing! I'll never forget it—baseball is a wonderful thing...

I hear as a tour guide, every day, "What a neat job you've got! What do you have to do to get this job?" You just have to be at the right place at the right time and be lucky! Everybody thinks it's a nice job and it is! There are a lot of people who are not as blessed, who are at nursing homes or who are shut-ins at their homes—I thank the Lord everyday that I'm allowed to be doing this at the end of my life. How many people get to do what would be their dream fantasy if they could write anything down they want to do and do it every day? I've missed one ball game in the last 11 years.

JOE BUCK* was at the park prior to the All-Star Game in 2009. I had a group of about 35 kids sitting in the green Cardinal Club seats because it is busy and we're waiting to take our turn to get out on the warning track to go to the dugout. Joe Buck was on the mound with several MLB people and they're shooting a commercial. When it's over, we're still in our seats and Joe Buck is walking out, exiting the field right by us. I say, "Hey, Joe! Could the kids say 'hi' and just get a picture of you?" Joe stopped, took my microphone and he asked the kids, "Are you having a good time? How's your tour going?" He was just as nice as he could be and we took a picture with him. He knew, because he is a smart guy, that Busch Stadium tour guides say,

---

*In 1996 **JOE BUCK**, at the age of twenty-seven, became the youngest national announcer on a World Series game. Previously, Sean McDonough in 1992 was the youngest at age thirty.

"You can't go on the grass. You have to stay on the warning track." So he says, "Now when you guys get ready to go over to the dugout, could you do me a favor? We're going to film something. Could you run across the infield grass to get to the dugout?" That's his humor! He looked at me and gave me a wink and went on his way! He left me to explain to the kids that "No", we really can't go across the infield grass but that's Joe Buck, and he's a neat, funny guy.

At another tour, we were all in the broadcast booth looking out at this majestic view of Busch Stadium. We were talking about why the Cardinals don't sell some of the seats out in center-field where that grassy knoll is so we could get more revenue and sign more players. We talked about the Batter's Eye Club, which is just beyond the grassy knoll in center field. One little third grade girl was on her toes, waving her hand and she says, "I know! I know! I know why they don't!" I said, "Okay." She says, "Mr. Jay, that's where the Cardinal players bury their dead pets!" Everybody roared!

Whenever **STAN MUSIAL*** makes an appearance at the park, the place gets electric! Because of his lack of mobility, he'll usually be on a cart going around the warning track. I always watch the visitor's dugout. You can watch all these young athletes, on any team, and they'll come out of that dugout and try to get as close as they can. They'll try to shake his hand because they know he is one of the greatest players that ever put on a uniform. Stop and think about what it says on that statue..."Here stands baseball's perfect warrior. Here stand baseball's perfect knight." 3630 hits...2nd to Ty Cobb and he's still 4th today. If you were ever in his presence, right now, he'll whip out his harmonica to play "Take Me Out to the Ballgame"... he's a true ambassador of the sport.

---

*Only three players hold their team's career record for most singles, doubles, triples and home runs. Those three players are George Brett, Robin Yount and **STAN MUSIAL**.

One of the great things about being a tour guide is that you get to be around the Stadium year round. Fans are around the Stadium when it's hustling and bustling with 45,000 people. It's so amazing to see it in stone silence, when nobody is there, or to "hear" the quiet of the snow on top of the grass. You look around the stands and think to yourself of all the wonderful things that have happened between families, marriage proposals, arguments about "should he have pitched to this guy or should he not have pitched to this guy." I have been blessed in my retirement to be over at the Stadium now for eleven years. I have noticed that everybody in the ballpark leaves their troubles at the gate and they're smiling. If they are on a tour, they are smiling. If they are at the game, they are smiling. It's just something that brings out the positive side of life. It's the most wonderful place to work in the world!

DONNY BASEBALL

DON MARQUESS

Don Marquess is a tower of power in the St. Louis business community. Marquess Gallery is renowned for its incredible baseball photos. The two outstanding photos celebrating KMOX in this book were the result of ideas and creations of Marquess. He also has a vested interest in the marina business these days.

Several years ago, my brother and his wife were in town and they were leaving on a Sunday at noon. Susan, my wife, and I stood outside and said good-bye to them...it just took an incredible amount of time. My shoes were going out of style! It was a 1:15 Cardinal game and they ended up leaving at 12:45. Susan said, "I don't have time to get ready—just go by yourself!" I had a place where I always parked my car; as a matter of fact, the lady always puts a cone in the spot so nobody takes it. I got there at 1:05, pulled into my spot, and the attendant, Karen, was very chatty. She wanted to talk to me about a lot of things, but I was in a hurry to get into the Stadium because the game is ready to start. I finally get out of my car, and run to the Stadium! I get my usual two **HOT DOGS*** and a Diet Coke, and get to my seat just as the National Anthem was playing. I reach into my pocket and don't feel my car keys. I think at that time, "Well, maybe I dropped them outside the car."

It was a blistering hot day and I couldn't find my keys, but I had to watch the game anyway. Also, I had to meet this friend of mine from Arizona. He comes through St. Louis about once

*The Boston Red Sox sell one and a half million **HOT DOGS** every season—the most in the majors.

a year, and we always go to games together. He had called me earlier in the day from Kansas City. He had slipped in the hotel bathroom and cracked some of his ribs and said that he might be late for the game. It was obvious on the phone that he was in extreme pain. Plus, several years before at Dulles Airport, he'd had a terrible accident and had to walk with the use of a Louisville Slugger-style cane. He said, "I'm probably going to be late, and I'm not going to be able to talk very much during the game."

He shows up in the third inning and he can barely move. He doesn't even say hello as he sits down next to me. He makes this embarrassing grunting noise as he does so. Every time he moved, whether it was to buy a Coke from a vendor or to get up and go to the restroom, he made this horrible grunting noise. Because he was in so much pain, we hardly talked even though I hadn't seen him in a year. This goes on for about five or six innings. He made one particularly loud grunting noise, so I said to him in a stentorian voice so that the Cardinal fans near me could clearly hear, "Pardon me, sir. Did you get your seats from a friend or did you buy them from a scalper." This was said to indicate that I had no knowledge of who this Monica Seles of the world was. He just looked at me and he slowly said his first words of the day; "I will get you."

The game continues and it is unbearably hot. Finally, in the ninth inning he starts the second conversation of the day, "I'm in a lot of pain. Would you mind very much giving me a ride to my car?" What could I say? I mean, I couldn't say no to the guy, and it was only then was it that I started thinking, "Holy cow! Where are my keys?"

We had to slowly walk across the street to the parking lot where I always park. As we are walking toward the parking lot, I'm still looking for my keys. If I dropped them outside the car, somebody probably saw them—I have a $50,000 Lexus SUV...and stole my car. As I round the curve, I see my car is still there. "Oh, thank God." I am looking around the bottom of my car for the keys. I reached for the door handle. Surprisingly, the door popped open and this blast of ice cold air hits me in the face! My car was running, unlocked, downtown St. Louis in front of Busch Stadium for three and a half hours!...

It's a mess around the Stadium with the game getting out and it's very crowded with cars but I have a very good parking spot right across from the Stadium—100 feet from the gate. I acted like I was happy to give him a ride to his car, "Oh, alright." He grunts as he gets in my car and says, "Hang a left!" so I edge my way into traffic on Walnut. It took us five minutes to get up to the light at Broadway. He says, "Hang a right!" so I hang a right which takes us into a larger flow of traffic trying to get on I-64. We inch our way down two stop lights further south of the Stadium. "Hang a right!" I hang a right and traffic is a lot less, but there is still a lot. We get down to a stop sign and he tells me to hang another right. Now we're heading back towards the other side of the Stadium. We get up even with the Stadium and I'm wondering, "Where is he parked?" He responded, "Keep going straight ahead." I'm thinking, "This is taking forever...I gotta get gas" We get up to the other edge of the Stadium and he says, "Hang a right!" I don't cook chili this long. Now we're right back near where we started and he says, "Hang a left!" We go into my parking space where we just left a half hour ago and his parked car was right next to my parking space!

He climbed out of my SUV, turned around and looked at me with a ---- -eating grin and said, "Call it a whim, call it a wild guess, Donny Baseball, but most people take their car keys with them at a ballgame. Number two, don't ever be mean to a cripple and an orphan (he was 70 years old) and lastly, thanks for the cool ride to my car. Someday they'll write songs about you."

He winked, turned, left and I haven't seen him since.

And that's what I did during my summer vacation.

THE SIGN MAN COMETH

MARTY PRATHER

Marty Prather, better known as "The Sign Man", lives the good life in Springfield, Missouri. Prather moved there in 1981 from Dayton, Ohio, where he was both a Reds and Cardinals fan. Prather owns over a dozen Dominos franchises and is an ardent supporter of the Missouri State Bears.

Istarted going to the Cardinal games in 1983, right after they won the Series in '82. I used to think it was a long way to drive from Dayton to Cincinnati—45 miles for a ballgame. Now I'm driving 210 miles each way. I started with signs in '85 with just one simple sign that said "The Fat Lady Is Singing" when the Cardinals were up three games to one in the World Series. My dad saw me on TV down in Florida. I didn't get to see my dad very much because my family was spread out.

I went up to Kansas City and the Royal fans had signs that said, "The Fat Lady Has Laryngitis", "The Fat Lady Is Choking". One little lady said, "I'm the fat lady and I'm here to sing." I started this little bit of a banter back and forth with one sign and I started thinking that this could be fun. In '86, I started bringing signs for individual players like "St. Louis Will Always Be The Land of Oz". The whole sign thing went crazy in '87 when the Cardinals went back to the Series. That was a fun year for me because I went to Minnesota with a sign that said, "Take Me Outside To The Ballgame" since that was the first World Series ever played indoors. It made *Sports Illustrated* but they cut me off! My hands made it and my sign made it but that was it. I wrote them a letter and said, "I had two goals when the World Series started. One was for the Cardinals to win and the other was for me to make it into your fine publication. The Cards came up a bit short and thanks to your crop man, so did I. Please cancel my subscription." Then I wrote "P.S. Wait a minute, the **SWIMSUIT ISSUE*** is only three months away, keep them coming until then."

A buddy of mine named John Short paints the signs for me. I'm just the idea man. Over the years, I've made over 2,000 signs and each sign costs about three pizzas on the average. I try to trade out for pizzas as much as I possibly can. I've fed his family for 25 years and put his kids through college, I know that!

You get more laughs out of signs that make fun of the opposing team than you do out of stuff like "Deep Freese Warning" and "The Cardinals Are Rockin' and Rollin'". It's the ones that play on the other team's shortcomings that are the best. I had one when Barry Bonds was going for Hank Aaron's record. He was about ten home runs away, so the media wasn't really covering it yet. I had this huge plastic Cardinal helmet from an Anheuser-Busch display. I made it into a San Francisco Giant helmet and I put Styrofoam in it. The circumference was four feet around. I wore it like I was a bobblehead. I had to buy a ticket for the helmet—to get it in. I had to have an extra seat so I'd have someplace to store it. The security people said, "Marty, no one behind this helmet is going to be able to see around it." I said, "I'm not going to wear it during the game, I'm just going to wear it during batting practice." They trusted me, and I kept my word, but it was funny. I walked around Busch Stadium with it and a sign that says, "Hey, Barry. I Found Your Helmet." He was sitting in the batting cage getting ready to take batting practice. I was behind the dugout and he looked over at me and smiled and said, "How much for the helmet?" I said, "You can have it!" He said, "What??" I said, "You just have to wear it

---

* *Sports Illustrated* first published in 1954 and its first swimsuit issue was in 1964. The *Sports Illustrated* **SWIMSUIT ISSUE** has 52 million readers, 16 million of them are females…12 million more than normal.

for a photo." He told me, "That's not going to happen." I said in return, "Are you afraid it won't fit?" He was laughing! He said, "That's obscene." When he goes into the Hall...which we all hope not...I'll be in **COOPERSTOWN*** with my helmet...

I've never had any trouble with security, but obviously, the signs can't be vulgar. Early on, they did check through my things to make sure they were appropriate for families. Now they just trust me. Brandon Phillips called the Cardinals a "bunch of b——-". When I walked in, they said, "Do you have any signs for Brandon Phillips?" I did but I said, "No." They said, "Okay. We just don't' want to stir anything up." I did bring one that said "Bob Barker said Brandon Phillips should be spayed or neutered" but I didn't hold it up.

My favorite Cardinal sign is probably "That's a Winner!" because I never held it up until the Cardinals had the game in hand. Getting close to Ozzie, I really like, "St. Louis Will Always Be The Land of Oz." The one I had for Harry Caray was good too. It said, "This Is Your Announcer." It had a picture of Harry sitting there. Then it said, "This Is Your Announcer On Bud" with a picture of Harry going crazy. I took it up to the press box to show him and the girl up there said, "I've got good news and I've got better news. The good news is that he signed it for you twice!" I said, "What's the better news?" She said, "Harry knew your name!" I have that **HARRY CARAY*** sign hanging in my basement. He wrote, "To Marty, Holy Cow!"

*Emmett Ashford, the first black umpire in Major League history, made it to **COOPERSTOWN**. His ashes are interred in the Lakewood Cemetery there.

*In the 1962 three-game playoff between the Giants and the Dodgers, **HARRY CARAY** did the local color on the San Francisco broadcast with Lon Simmons and Russ Hodges.

I had a sign for Gary Carter that said, "Carter Couldn't Throw Out The Trash." That's when Vince Coleman and all the guys were stealing wild back in the '80s. Carter came over and autographed it...laughingly. I had one for Mitch Williams that said, "Mild Thing. You Make Our Bats Sing". He autographed it. I met Will Clark when he had that short stint with the Cardinals and had a sign that said, "Will's a Thrillin', Champagne's a Chillin'". At the All-Star Game in St. Louis, a guy walked up to me and said, "Hey. I really appreciate what you do with your signs." He had sunglasses and a ball cap on. I said, "Really? Where do you live now?" He took off his sunglasses and said, "I'm Will Clark. I appreciated you even in '87 when we were playing against you in the playoffs...just your enthusiasm and what you bring to the ballpark." It's nice words like that that keeps me doing this.

One of my signs that got the most coverage was just a simple one. it was right after 9/11. It was eerie just walking into the ballpark. You didn't know whether to cheer or applaud or cry or what. It was just awkward; very uncomfortable. Then Jack Buck read that dramatic poem, and you knew that was the place you wanted to be. Baseball helped bring America back a little bit. I had a sign that said, "Baseball Has Players. America Has Heroes". With all the fancy signs and artwork I've had, I got more compliments on that sign. It made the front page of the *Dayton Daily News.* My dad was back in Dayton and called me up crying. Dad was a paratrooper in **WORLD WAR II***. He said, "I didn't realize you were that patriotic." I said, "Just because I didn't serve, Dad, doesn't mean that I don't appreciate those of you that did." It was a pretty special moment for me and my dad....

*The first American off the boats on **D-DAY** at Normandy was actor James Arness, later of "Gunsmoke" fame. The reason Arness was the first was he was the tallest soldier on the first boat to land and the Admiral wanted to measure how deep the water was.

I started collecting when I was three years old. My dad took me to Crosley Field and I got a pennant. When I talk to young people, I tell them, "Find something that you love. Don't collect it for monetary purposes. Find something that you like and you want to display." I have 280 different Cardinal pennants on my ceiling. It takes eight to make a semi-circle and I'm already out of wall space. I've got pennants from the '30s to the current day thumb-tacked into my ceiling. I've got a scorecard from every year from '34 on for the Cardinals. The ones from the '50s are beautiful with all the artwork. The Cardinals have started going back to that in the past few years. I've got every press pin for every Cardinals World Series other than '31. The toughest ones to find are from '42 and '43 because that was during the war years and they were oversized. They weren't actually embossed into the metal. They were covered in paper, and after the game was over, they took the paper off and melted the pin back down for the war effort. If you ever see a '42 or '43 press pin, snag it, because they are few and far between. I have programs from every World Series the Cardinals have ever played in from '26 through 2011.

I built a **DUGOUT*** in my basement. It was my wife's gift for my 50th birthday—she approved the plan! It encloses the couch so that when you're on the couch, you're actually inside the dugout watching the game on the big screen. On the outside, I've got a riser built on both sides. I got eight seats from Busch built on the risers so that you can put your beer on top of the dugout and watch the game.

About the most favorite collectible—like the '42-'43 pins—is a little five dollar glass that I got from a Stadium giveaway in

*When the Astrodome opened in 1965, it had the first ever corporate luxury boxes (Sky Boxes)...The Astrodome also had the longest **DUGOUTS** in baseball history...The owner, Judge Hofheinz, knew that most people loved sitting behind dugouts. This, of course, allowed him to charge premium prices for these extra "dugout seats" behind the elongated dugout.

Crosley Field when I was six years old. My mom told me, "Don't take that to school for show and tell, you might break it." I took it anyway. I broke it. She said, "We just can't have nice things." I was in Cleveland walking through the National Card show and there was the glass! It had **MR. REDLEG*** on it. I asked how much it was. It was marked five dollars at the bottom. I said, "I would have given $500!" The guy said, "Well, you still can!" I told him that was okay...five dollars is good!" When I started collecting things, my wife would ask me how much something was. I'd tell her fifty bucks. She'd say, "It was a hundred." I said, "How did you know that?" She said, "You always just cut it in half. You've always done that." Now I just tell her everything is five dollars. I brought in an old seat from Sportsman's Park. She said, "What's that?" I said, "It's an old seat from Sportsman's Park, you know, the ballpark before Busch." She said, "Five dollars?" I said, "No, Honey, this was ten." We're going to be married 25 years soon. She'll probably keep me around until she gets the radio fixed.

My life doesn't revolve around the Cardinals, but it is what we do for entertainment. We get treated well by all the people at Busch. It's like a second family to me. When you see people that you only see at the ballpark and you can walk up and say, "Hi!" it's almost like walking into a Cheers episode. When you're there and the ushers come over and say, "Hi!" and the fans and the players wave at you, it's like a home away from home.

When I see the kids in the minors here in Springfield, and they end up with the big team, I realize that the big leagues don't

---

*In April of 1957, Don Hoak of the **REDS** was on second base and Gus Bell was on first when Wally Post hit a double-play ground ball. Hoak fielded the ball with his bare hands and tossed the ball to Johnny Logan, the shortstop for the Milwaukee Braves. Hoak was automatically out for interference—but not the batter—and Hoak thereby avoided an easy double-play. The Reds did that three times that year before the rule was changed.

change people. They are who they are. Money doesn't change true, genuine people. Dave Freese hasn't changed one iota from when he was here. Colby Rasmus is still the country kid from Alabama. He's a nice guy, and I wish him well in Toronto. There are some guys that have a little bit of an entitlement attitude. Some of them even have it here. I don't see people change. They're already formed by the time they get to the big leagues.

I was lucky to have moved to Missouri thirty years ago.

HE'S FROM THE QUAD CITIES; IT'S TWICE AS GOOD AS THE TWIN CITIES

STEVE SPURGETTIS

Steve Spurgettis, 50, grew up in East Moline, IL, a "suburb: of the Quad Cities (Davenport and Bettendorf, Iowa and Moline and Rock Island, IL). The Quad Cities once had an NBA team called the Tri-City Black-hawks coached by Red Auerbach. That team moved to Milwaukee and a few years later moved again and became the St. Louis Hawks. The Quad Cities is 270 miles north of St. Louis. Spurgettis lives in Florissant, MO and works for Frito Lay.

In 2011, my friend and I didn't have a ticket for Game 6 of the World Series. We met up with some friends of his that were tailgating in the parking lot right outside of Busch Stadium. We had the game on the radio while we were tailgating, but we could hear the actual crowd reactions. Outside center field, if you're looking inside Busch Stadium, there was a monitor where you could watch the game from the outside of the Stadium!

My best recollection of the whole thing was Freese's home run. You could see the ball getting hit on the screen, and then you look up above and actually see the ball in its flight above Busch Stadium. It looked like a meteor coming right at us, it was too cool! Then it disappeared and the place went crazy!...

There was a time when Anheuser-Busch didn't own the team so the Clydesdales weren't really a part of the pageantry that took place on opening day or the playoffs. The last day at old Busch Stadium was the first time in quite a few years that the Clydesdales came onto the field. We had seats in left field up in the second level. I went down to the rail to take some pictures when they played the traditional Budweiser "Here Comes the King" music! If you've ever tried to take a picture of the Clydesdales, you know how hard it is to get a good photo of all the horses. Remember back in the '80s, whenever they would bring the wagon onto the field, Gussie Busch would be up on top with his famous red cowboy hat. This time, they had that hat in a glass case sitting up on top of the Anheuser-Busch wagon! In the past, the wagon and Clydesdales had always rolled right through and left the Stadium but that day it parked in front of the Cardinals dugout between home and first. All those players that had been out on the field lined up like a "team photo" in front of it! When the Clydesdales left through the wagon gate, they disappeared right underneath a sign that referenced **KMOX*** and the memories at Busch Stadium being priceless—it was a nice closing ceremony....

***KMOX** went on the air on Christmas Eve in 1924 in Kirkwood, MO. KMOX operated only three days a week—Mondays, Thursdays and Sundays.

I helped coach a baseball team with a couple buddies of mine. They were the main coaches. These kids were nine years old. They started practicing at an indoor batting cage in January. They would do drills, play catch inside the batting cage, in addition to pitching and hitting. One night in January, they were about to wind down the practice—they had about 20 minutes left on the two cages. The man who runs the place, walked over to Mark, the head coach, "Hey Mark, I have a guy that wants to come in and hit, would you mind moving over into one cage?" Mark said, "Well, we're just about to wrap it up so I think we can do that. We're only going to do a couple more things." Unexpectedly, the door opens and the cold air blows in. In walks in this guy wearing shorts, a black zip-up jacket and a baseball cap pulled down real low. The kids stared at him as he walked into the cage. He was wearing a cut-off, sleeveless t-shirt and some **JORDAN*** basketball shorts. They realized then that it was Albert Pujols....in January...on a Friday night!

The kids started to get excited seeing Albert and they started paying more attention to Albert than their coaches. The guy that was with Albert said, "He's not going to sign any auto-graphs, but if you guys want to pull up a chair and watch him hit, you can."

So these 15 kids pull their chairs right up next to the batting cage. Albert took ten minutes of soft toss with the rubber batting cage balls, then he proceeded to go against live pitching with regular baseballs. The sound inside this building was like nothing you had ever heard. You always hear about big sluggers and big hitters creating a unique sound with the bat when it hits the ball, but this was indoors! It was like lightning striking inside...it was loud and thunderous!

*In 1994, the Chicago White Sox recalled **MICHAEL JORDAN** from Double-A Birmingham to play against the Chicago Cubs in the Mayor's Trophy Game at Wrigley Field. Jordan singled and doubled against the Cubs.

So here are these nine-year-old kids watching Albert taking batting practice....inside...in January, when he could have been out at a club or with his friends and family. Instead, he's inside at a batting cage in January working on his hitting. He hit for about forty minutes.

I told my buddy, "There is nothing that the four of us could teach these kids this whole year better than what they just learned tonight. That's the best lesson that they'll ever learn... that a guy, who is MVP caliber, is inside at a batting cage on a Friday night, working on his hitting. He had a great season and we were able to tell all of those kids, "That's how you get better. You work on your hitting...dedicate yourself and you will get results."

SHORT STORIES FROM LONG MEMORIES

My job as the full-time batting practice pitcher for the St. Louis Cardinals is a dream job. I have been a Cardinal fan since I was four years old. Back in the '50s, the Cardinals weren't very good, but they were still my team—my heroes. My dad would take me out into the bleachers in left field underneath the big scoreboard. I didn't know where the heck Busch Stadium was, but I knew it was a magical place!

In 2001, I had a chance to try out for the St. Louis Cardinal batting practice pitcher job on an invitation from Dave McKay. I ended up getting lost going into Busch Stadium. I was awe-struck at that time. Since then, I have learned that they are just normal guys and like to be treated as such.

The first guys I threw to were Fernando Vina, Edgar Renteria, J.D. Drew and Placido Polanco. I was scared to death like anyone would have been. After throwing a few strikes like I did to my high school kids for 35 years, I remember J.D. Drew saying, "This guy's okay—we can hit off him. Let's give him a chance!" So I owe J.D. Drew a lot! In 2006, the Cardinals asked me if I wanted to go on the road with them. I've been on every road trip, every spring training game, everything since I retired from teaching. That's my story!

I liked Drew and Vina. They were real down-to-earth guys! I'd see them over at Paddy O's after a game, and they'd treat me like one of the guys in the clubhouse! Vina was especially good to me—I really liked him. I felt sorry for Drew. He just never panned out as the player they thought he would be. He's a really good guy. Everybody was down on him all the time but I really enjoyed hanging around with him.

—**Dennis Schutzenhofer**, Fairview Heights, IL; Retired teacher and coach. Batting practice pitcher for the Cardinals.

My dad used to work at the Stadium. We would sit in the box seats for batting practice and would walk out of there with a lot of balls from batting practice. Back then the **BATTING CAGES*** were about half the size of the cages they use now.

My favorite player is still Lou Brock. Brock was the pioneer of having music played for the players as they came up to bat. They used to play the, "*The Theme From Shaft*" when he batted. "Doot a doot, doot a doot, DOOVE" He was the very first player that they ever did that for. I don't remember songs being played for any of the other players then—only Brock.

I saw Lou Brock get his 3,000th hit against the Cubs. He hit that line drive off of Dennis Lamp's finger, breaking his finger. It wasn't sold out—maybe a crowd of 25,000. We were out at the left field wall right by the foul pole. It was neat to stand at the railing overlooking the field. It was really breathtaking. Back then, the Cards used to give out certificates you had to fill in yourself saying, "I was there when..." I got one for his 3000th hit and ended up giving it to my nephew. He later got it autographed by Lou himself!

I worked as an usher at Busch Stadium from '76-'79. Those were the years that were lean. There was hardly anybody going to the games. It wasn't like it is now, where it's packed every night. Back then, the field box would be three sections going down to the corner in both right and left field and it would be closed off. They were empty. There would be no one there. Sometimes the upper deck would be empty. We had to stand there to keep the stragglers from trying to get up there.

When baseball started in April, we would wear blue blazers until sometime in May. Then, for the summer months we would wear the red and white candy striped shirts with the blue pants that had the little red stripe going down the side. When the weather would start cooling off again, we would wear the blue blazers again.

---

*Forbes Field in Pittsburgh was so huge that the Pirates would store the **BATTING PRACTICE CAGE** on the grass in distant center field.

I always liked the scoreboard that would light up when the Cardinals hit a home run. The bird would whistle or sing as it was coming around and would land on the clock. That was an awesome thing to see. It would really be neat if they would bring that back.

In 2009, the evening of the All-Star Game, I took my boat and went fishing on the Mississippi while listening to the game on my radio. I was just north of the Arch, just fishing and enjoying my two favorite pastimes. Me and my dad used to spend many nights at Carlyle Lake listening to Jack Buck and Mike Shannon. When I was in high school, Dad would take me fishing on Lake Taneycomo, near Branson. A lot of times, we would see Darrell Porter and Whitey Herzog out there fishing too! I tell you what, I do miss calling Dad up and just going fishing while we listen to the ballgame.

—**John White III**, Florissant, MO, Boeing Retiree

Opening day has always been a tradition for us. It was the first year that we had camped out for the 550 KTRS First Pitch tickets, and there were severe thunderstorms due to come through the St. Louis area. We had to run back to the car to get a few things, and just as soon as we got to the car, the storms came rolling in. From what the news reports said, there was an F1 category tornado somewhere downtown. We had seen a port-a-potty go blowing by...still standing straight up. It slid about one hundred and fifty to two hundred feet—right down 8th Street. In all my days at Busch Stadium, I never thought I'd see a port-a-potty go sliding past the big Musial statue. My girlfriend had to hunker down in our tent just to keep the tent from blowing away. Some random lady ran into the tent to help her hold it down. We were over to the right side of the Stadium, directly behind home plate if you are facing the Stadium. The tent was directly in front of the stands so she almost went for a ride! What a day...

My girlfriend bought me a **STAN THE MAN*** jersey from an antique store. It's a child-size uniform from the early 1950's and it's autographed by Stan. I have it in a glass case. It's awesome! It's a kid's uniform...pants, shirt and hat...that someone had bought from Famous-Barr years ago. Most people that see it have never seen anything like it. It's all hand-stitched with the old Birds on the Bat. It has an authentic look to it but it is a miniature version. Musial signed the jersey and hat. He wrote, "Hall of Fame—69." That was the year he was inducted into the Hall of Fame. It's my pride and joy.

—**Will Gardner**,St. Charles, MO, Mechanic

All through high school and college, I always wanted to have season tickets. On the first day after I got out of college, I heard an ad about the Cardinals selling season tickets in the bleachers for the first time. I thought it would be pretty cool to get in those seats right in the beginning. I went with my future wife and a friend of mine from college and we bought four seats in the bleachers. We were trying to get left field bleachers on the aisle next to the Cardinals bullpen. We thought we had those

***STAN MUSIAL** never struck out three times in a game until his very last season at the age of forty-two when Dick Ellsworth of the Cubs performed the feat.

seats until a couple weeks later when the ticket office called me and said, "We're sorry, those seats have been sold already and we've moved you over to row two in the right field bleachers." We were bummed! We really didn't want to be on that side. It turned out great though. What they called "row two" was actually "row one" because they had moved the walls. Then during the **MCGWIRE*** years—'98-'99—they ended up moving the Cardinal bullpen from left field to right field so we did end up being next to the Cardinals' bullpen! We've also been in the front row ever since 1997. It all worked out perfectly.

We've been taking mainly family to the Cardinal games-my wife and I, both of our Dads and now our son who was born in '05. We used to have four seats. In our row at the old Stadium there were twelve seats, however, at the new Stadium they squeezed in a thirteenth seat. To be honest, it upset us at first because we had our routine set! The guy on the end towards the bullpen had eight seats and we had our four; that's our 12 seats. When they added the 13th seat, they sold the single seat that was between us. Well, I guess that single seat was really meant for our son because eventually, the person who had that single seat bailed out and we were able to acquire that fifth seat! Now the three of us can go with our two dads. There was a reason they added that 13th seat at the new Stadium! It was meant to be.

Obviously, being a lifelong Cardinal fan and having a wife who is also a fan, we have a collection of Cardinal things. Our best piece of memorabilia is a seven foot section of the back wall from the old Busch Stadium visitors dugout that we purchased when the old Stadium closed. There were stains all over it and the first thing she wanted to do when we got it home

*In the late '90s, the Cardinals commissioned a statue of Mark **MCGWIRE** that is currently stored inside Busch Stadium....When Mark McGwire was a senior in high school, he was drafted as a pitcher by the Montreal Expos in the eighth round...when Patriots quarterback Tom Brady was a senior in high school, he was drafted by the Expos in the twelfth round as a catcher.

was to clean it. Absolutely not! There is no way that will ever get cleaned! The Cardinals also gave season ticket holders the opportunity to buy their old seats, so we have our old bleachers from the old Stadium. It's just a couple chunks of wood, but we know what it is and what it means!

Baseball is just so much more than a game. In St. Louis, it's comparable to a religion. You see old friends and you become friends with your ushers because you're sitting in the same spot all of the time. People in St. Louis just love baseball, love the Cardinals, and love going to the Cardinals games. We are lucky to be in St. Louis.

—**John Reed**, 38, Millstadt, IL

My sister Ruth got married at the ballpark on May 22, 2006. She told people, "Yeah come to the wedding! It's fine! There are plenty of seats!" It ended up being really hot that day! By the time the wedding started it got a little shady, thankfully! It was only May 22nd and it was 90 degrees! Fredbird drove my brother-in-law and the best man in his little car out to home plate. My mother and sister walked out from the seats out to the pitcher's mound. That's where they actually got married—at the pitcher's mound. Their names were on the big screen and fireworks went off. That was very cool!

—**Mindy Bates**, Originally from Granite City, IL.
Resides in St. Louis, MO

Back when I was in high school, money was pretty short but we still liked to go to the Cardinal games. A really good friend of mine, Kenny May, and I used to work at McDonald's together. On the days we weren't working at McDonald's we would usually decide to go down to the game... with no money. One of the ways we got into the baseball game was to wait until about the fourth inning when the gates opened up. That was a good way to do it! Back in '88-'90, the Cardinals weren't the greatest. When the gates opened, we would sneak in. In the old Busch Stadium, you had to have a red ticket stub to get down low...you couldn't just walk down low and sit by the dugout. Usually people would leave from down below because they had had enough. They would walk out of the Stadium and we'd ask them for the stubs so we could go down by the field. Sure enough we would get a couple! We would go and see a good half of the game sitting down in the box seats. We didn't have to pay for a ticket and we'd have enough money for a hot dog and a soda! We would either sit in an open seat or sit in the seats of whoever gave us the ticket stubs. There was maybe only one time we got chased out by the ushers—there were plenty of seats down there and usually everybody was a pretty good sport about it...

—**Jeff Evans**, Brighton, IL

In June, 2002, after Jack Buck passed away, fans gathered around the Jack Buck statue at the Stadium and laid down t-shirts, hats, flowers, balloons, flags...anything patriotic or Cardinal-related. Some people had written notes. This make-shift memorabilia pile grew and grew. People would just stand there and stare at it for a long time. Police officers guarded it overnight. There were candles lit all around it. We were standing there one afternoon and it was really quiet. You could hear all kinds of buzzing up around the Stadium but it was silent by the memorial.

As people came out of the glass doors where the media and players would exit, they would walk past and take a look to see how big it had grown. There was a man with his son. The man was a little emotional and teary eyed as his wife was behind him rubbing his back. They're talking and pointing things out when all of a sudden—while looking at the statue, the little boy—around four years old—says, "Dad, why is he frozen?" He thought the statue was a person that was frozen! His mom whispered to him, "It's not like Star Wars." There is a scene in Star Wars where Hans Solo gets frozen...I guess that's what the boy was talking about! We laughed...

—**Ken Leonard**, Hannibal, MO

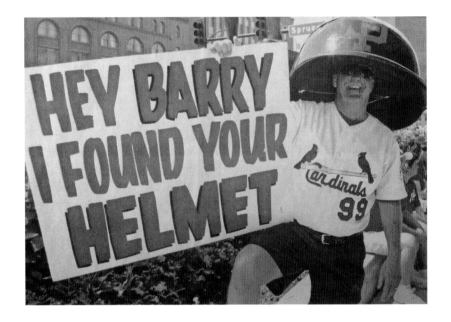

Chapter Three

ON THE ROAD AGAIN

We're Gonna Follow The Cardinals Till Hell Freezes Over...Then We're Gonna Follow 'Em On Ice

LEWIS LEVEY ONCE HAD AN ARM WRESTLING BET WITH CLARK KENT. THE LOSER HAD TO WEAR HIS UNDERWEAR OUTSIDE HIS PANTS

LEWIS LEVEY

Lewis Levey is a towering figure in both commercial real estate and St. Louis social circles. From Cardinal Fantasy Camps to Michael Jordan's Fantasy Camp to going to the White House with the Cardinals in 2012, Levey continues to live out every sports fan's childhood dreams...and he's a nice guy to boot.

The **WHITE HOUSE*** invitation came in a phone call about five days before the White House ceremony. We had to give them security information, driver's license and other data for clearance. I was in West Palm Beach, Florida and to get to Washington I had to get up at 4:30 in the morning for an early flight out of Ft. Lauderdale. My wife and I met the team in D.C. and went to the White House. My wife and I got separated because we were mingling. They wouldn't let us go in separately.

We met outside the east entrance to the White House. I came in a suit and had four World Series balls that I took to get signed.

When **PRESIDENT Harry Truman died in 1972, archivists found his 1968 Busch Stadium Pass for the baseball Cardinals...Truman also owned part of the Rams, investing $45, 000 in 1958. He later sold off $20,000 of his investment. He declared the Rams interest income on his taxes from 1959 to 1963. The highest dividend paid by the Rams was $1,486 in 1959.*

There were three levels of security getting into the White House. We were all queued up—the team wasn't—but the 50 others of us attending and the media were. We got through one security level, got through a second level and all the way to the third tier of security, when they said, "No baseballs." To make it worse, they said I could leave the balls there but we couldn't reclaim them. I wanted to have the President and some of the players sign them. I forfeited the balls as did a few people. The security acted like it could be a "thrown missile". But—they did let people bring in bats! A lady who was about five people behind me, had a full box of balls. I don't know if they were World Series or just regular game balls, but it was a full box. I'm sure these Secret Service guys took those balls home or maybe took them in after we left and had them signed. I'm glad I went to the White House, but it wasn't off the charts good. After we got into the White House, there was a military band playing St. Louis songs, the Budweiser song and other neat songs. There were drinks and appetizers, and we lollygagged around awhile.

We were in the auditorium that had chairs and a temporary dais. There were about 100 people there. The President was late. Instead of starting at 2:30, it started at ten minutes to three. Meanwhile, the television stations are all there beaming it back to St. Louis. That's when my buddies were all texting me telling me—"Bad tie", "Show more of your left side, not your right"— that kind of thing. It was fun. The Cardinals gave both Michelle and the **PRESIDENT*** a jersey with their names on it. He made some comments and DeWitt made some comments, Berkman made comments...It was a fun deal. After it was over, we mingled around with the players. They would have signed autographs except I didn't have the baseballs anymore. The players were all gone in about 20 minutes...

*The Army head football coach makes three times as much money as the **PRESIDENT** of the United States.

HE'S BEEN A CARDINAL FAN EVER SINCE GEORGE HENDRICK HAMMED IT UP FOR THE FANS BY SLIGHTLY ARCHING HIS LEFT EYEBROW

STEVE ROSEBROUGH

Along with Earl Kaplan, Steve Rosebrough helped build Books Are Fun *of Fairfield, Iowa into a conglomerate that was purchased by* Readers Digest *a decade ago for tens of millions of dollars. Rosebrough moved to Boulder, Colorado where he is currently Vice President of Purchasing and Publisher for* Imagination Books. *Rosebrough's story is one of using baseball to reconnect with important family members.*

When I was seven years old, my dad took me to my first Cardinals game. He was so excited to take me, however the Braves won 14-1...the Cardinals just got blown out of the water. He said, "Okay, that can't be your first game experience, try and erase that from your memory." We went back the next night and it was 0-0 in the bottom of the ninth when Silent George Hendrick hit a solo shot to win the game at 1-0. We were sitting out in left field and the ball landed a couple of rows in front of me. Ever since then, I've been hooked on baseball...on Cardinal baseball. My parents got divorced and my dad moved down to Florida. I didn't get to spend a lot of time with him growing up, but one of the common bonds that we had is that we always talked baseball...

My dad had been attending Cardinal Fantasy Camps and he said to me, "Steve, now that you're 30, I would really like to do a Cardinal Fantasy Camp with you." I said, "Okay, I'll do it someday." Then, he had a very serious stroke. After that I said, "Alright Dad, I'll do this Cardinals Camp with you now." I was really afraid that I would never have another chance to do it with him.

The next year, after he recovered and was cleared to play ball, we went to the Fantasy Camp together. At the camp, each camper is put on a team, and each team is managed by a retired Cardinal. My dad and I ended up in the Championship Game that year. When I hit the game-winning home run, my dad was waiting for me at home plate. There is a great picture of me crossing home plate and running into my dad's arms... it's pretty powerful.

Steve Rosebrough is hugged by his father after hitting game-winning home run.

It's never too late to rekindle those important relationships. *"Carpè Diem"*....seize the day! You never know when the people you love are going to leave the world, so you want to spend that time with them....take every chance you can. It was so cool because I never had the chance to grow up with my dad. He lived hundreds of miles away, so to be able to share that baseball moment with my dad was pretty awesome. All sports are amazing, but baseball, at least for our family, is a real way to heal.

A couple of days before this game-winning home run, I was in the batting cage receiving hitting instructions from Silent George Hendrick so it all came full circle. George hit that game-winning home run, back when I was seven years old and here he was instructing me, only for me to hit the game winner—it was unreal!

I thought it was going to be cool just hanging with my dad and the Cardinal players and playing ball, but half of the fun was hearing these guys' stories—the behind the scene stories, the hardships, the fun, the camaraderie, the joking, the locker room antics. That stuff is pretty cool!

I became closest to Lou Brock—he's become a family friend. I invited him to my grandmother's 90th birthday in the Owners' Box at Busch Stadium. Then he invited my family to his 72nd birthday, also in the Owners' Box. All of Busch Stadium, turned and sang *Happy Birthday* to him...and under his arm was my son Hunter. Lou is just a super nice guy. He can still hit the heck out of the ball. He is just pure heart and is all about family, all about giving back to the community. He and his wife Jackie are just phenomenal people. I feel really privileged to have him in my life, even in a small way.

The guy that I had the most fun with at the camps was Danny Cox. He likes to drink a beer or two so he's really fun to hang with. The one that I love to antagonize, even though he likes to throw at my head and give me some "chin music" is Todd

Worrell. I shared a glove in center field with Vince Coleman. He forgot his glove one day so when it was his turn to field, I would just drop my glove in center and he would run out and use it.

Whitey Herzog used to come to camp every year, but he hasn't been there the last few years. When Whitey started talking— and I kid you not—within the next twenty minutes there would be fifty to sixty people around that table, just trying to listen to Whitey. He's like a catalog of stories....an encyclopedia.

The fantasy camp was not only a great opportunity to actually spend time with my dad, it's been like a family reunion with all of my heroes. Ozzie Smith started coming the last two years and he adds so much to the mix. **BOB GIBSON*** has been there a couple years. He's intimidating. I wouldn't say he's all heart, he's still as tough as he was back in the day and he's got some good stories as well.

I couldn't go a year without it. There was one year that I didn't do the camp and I was depressed for six months. It's become an important part of my life.

***BOB GIBSON** played basketball with the Harlem Globetrotters several off-seasons....In 1972, Bill Cosby signed a lifetime contract with the Globetrotters for one dollar per year. In 1986, the Globetrotters gave him a nickel raise. Cosby made several appearances with the team and is an honorary member of the Basketball Hall of Fame.

NOTRE DAME NEEDS A FULLBACK, A HALFBACK, AND ARA BACK

DICK FOX

Dick Fox, 70, grew up on a farm near Lost Nation, Iowa, listening to Harry Caray and Jack Buck. He is now retired and lives on Cape Cod.

(Left: Dick Fox with Christie Vilsack, the wife of the Secretary of Agriculture)

I'm a Notre Dame graduate and the three top **NOTRE DAME*** media people in South Bend are all St. Louis Cardinal fans: Darin Pritchett of ESPN Radio, Jeff Jeffers the long-time, legendary sports anchorman in South Bend, and Eric Hansen, the *South Bend Tribune* beat writer for Notre Dame football. Every year, the group tries to take a Cardinals trip. In 2006, Eric Hansen and I went to the baseball All-Star Game in Pittsburgh. We got our tickets from Mike Reilly, who at that time had been a Major League umpire for 26 years. We get to our seats in the upper deck, down the left field line three rows from the top of the stadium. The next time we saw Mike Reilly we said, "Hey, Mike! If you umpire another 26 years in the Big Leagues, do you think you might be able to get us All-Star Game tickets six rows from the top of the stadium?" He said, "Yeah, I probably can, but in the meantime, who's going to get you those All-Star tickets in Yankee Stadium the year after next that you've been begging for?"

*The Oakland A's colors are green and gold colors because their late owner, Charles O. Finley, grew up in LaPorte, Indiana and loved **NOTRE DAME**...when he bought the Kansas City A's, he changed their uniforms to the Notre Dame colors...The Green Bay Packers also adopted the Notre Dame colors because Curly Lambeau played at Notre Dame.

Well, we didn't get tickets to that All-Star Game in **<u>YANKEE STADIUM</u>*** in 2008, but we did make it to a St. Louis Cardinals game at PNC Park in Pittsburgh that July. We had decent seats in the second deck. Saturday night, the Cardinals have a huge lead going into the ninth inning. I said, "Eric, we need to get down there in the high roller seats...that's where guys like us deserve to be." He said, "Yeah, you're right." Of course, being the Pirates at the time, the attendance was very sparse. It's the ninth inning and the Pirates were getting killed so we move down into the "A-list" seats. There is absolutely nobody in the section we are sitting in down low right by the field level...no one.

We sit down and within two minutes this black usher comes down and says, "Hey, you guys can't sit there." I look right at him, and for whatever reason and I know not whatever possessed me, I said, "Oprah said it was okay." The usher looks at us, turns around and leaves. We sat there as the Pirates rallied for like seven runs in the bottom of the ninth to beat us. Every time I call Eric Hansen, he says, "Does Oprah know that you're calling?"

Incidentally, Eric Hansen has been to many Cardinals games in St. Louis and on the road. At the two Busch Stadiums, he's been to 27 games and the Cardinals have won every single one of them....

The Cardinals sometimes have an international flavor. In 1967, my wife and I were vacationing at the Las Brisas Hotel in Acapulco. The Las Brisas was famous in those days because it was built on a hillside overlooking Acapulco Bay and each room had a small swimming pool. Each room also had a pink jeep

---

*Thomas Edison sold the concrete to the Yankees that was used to build **<u>YANKEE STADIUM</u>**. Edison owned the huge Portland Cement Company...Edison's middle name was Alva, named after the father of onetime Cleveland Indians owner, Alva Bradley.

with a pink and white canopy. My wife spied Tim McCarver* and his wife checking in.

Later, when McCarver paid the shoe shine boy, he gave him a hundred peso bill as a tip which was eight dollars in those days. I said to him, "Did you just realize you gave him an eight dollar tip?" He said, "No! I thought it was an eighty-cent tip!" We started talking and he told about how this was the first trip to Mexico, and asked if we had been there for a while. I told him we had been there for a week. He said, "Would you mind showing us some of the sights of the town?" McCarver was the player rep for the Cardinals, and had just finished player rep meetings in Mexico City.

That night we went out on the town. We had another couple with us, so there were three couples, but the jeep would only hold four people. **MCCARVER*** and I, in an absolutely stupid move, decided we were going to ride on the fenders of the jeep. Incredibly dumb in retrospect, but we're relatively young at the time and didn't think much of it. McCarver said to me, "What is the Spanish word for our "F" word?" I told him, "Cuchara." We're riding through downtown Acapulco, and we were yelling out, "Cuchara! Cuchara!" like Ugly Americans are wont to do. A couple of years later I found out that the word cuchara is Spanish for "spoon". It would be like some Mexicans riding on the fenders of a jeep in downtown St. Louis yelling, "Spoon! Spoon!" We were too young and too stupid at the time to realize how bad that was.

The next day, we were playing volleyball on the beach at the Acapulco Hilton Hotel. On the opposing team were these two girls just a little younger than we were. They were beautiful young ladies with very attractive figures and wearing bikinis that made their cleavage look like an entrance to a major recreational area. After playing for about 20 minutes,

*TIM MCCARVER debuted with the Cardinals in 1959. In August 1961, he was "demoted" to the minors in order to remove him from the expansion player pool draft for the newly formed Mets and Astros.

MCCARVER* came over, grabbed me by the elbow and said, "Listen. When you throw that ball across the net to the other team, make sure you throw it only to those two girls and you throw it knee high." I started to ask why, but then I realized what he was getting at. We played for another half hour while Tim's wife at the time, Ann, was sitting over on the sidelines with my wife. She says, "Timmy, honey. Could you come here for a second?" Tim marches over. In the player rotation, I happened to be closest on that side of the court where the wives were sitting. McCarver's wife said in a much lower tone, "Timmy, if you throw that ball knee high to either of those two girls again, I am going to go up to the room. I'm going to start packing and I'll meet you back in Memphis."...

Fast forward ahead quite a few years, and in 2003, I'm on the St. Louis Cardinals Winter Cruise. That particular year, the cruise went to the Caribbean islands. One day we sail into Montego Bay. Now, in my mind over all those years, I always thought that Montego Bay was going to be this gorgeous, sand-swept resort area, with crystal blue water and just beautiful sights. Just before the boat docked, several of the Cardinal celebrities including Mike Matheny, said, "Hey! We're going over to Jimmy Buffett's Margaritaville, why don't you come with us?" I said, "I have some work that will take me at least an hour, but I'll meet you over there." I came off the boat an hour later, and I'm greeted by all these young men who wanted to be my "guide" for the day. Since I knew where I was going, I had no use for a guide. I pulled out a dollar bill and said, "Alright, here is my budget for a guide for the day—it's one dollar." I pointed to a guy and said, "You can be my guide, and when I have used up a dollar's worth of your time, you can just be on your way." We went to downtown Montego Bay to the post office and it was dreadful. It was smelly and just terrible. I decided that maybe Margaritaville was going to be like that, too.

***Brent Musburger was the home plate umpire when TIM MCCARVER made his pro baseball debut for Keokuk, Iowa, in the Midwest League in 1959.**

I told the guide that I just wanted a cab back to the boat. Perhaps he was getting a commission from the taxi driver because he jumped into the cab with us. We have about a four mile ride out to the dock area. We were nearing the dock and, in fact, I could see our cruise ship anchored about a mile off shore. About the same time, I saw four dogs dart out from the right side of the cab going lickity-split across the road. Then I realized they weren't slowing down which meant they weren't going to bark at the tires of the cab, they were chasing something that was in the ditch to the left side of the cab.

WOMP! THUMP! The cab hit those dogs so hard, it almost tipped the cab over and it killed two of the dogs. Whereupon, my guide went berserk! He started screaming at the cabbie, "You have killed my grandmother!" Obviously, he believed in reincarnation, and thought one of those dogs was his grandmother. The other dog might have been Shirley Maclaine. It looked like the cabbie and my "guide" were going to kill each other. I'm looking at the cruise liner a mile out to sea, Although I can't swim, I could probably have walked 2/3 of the way out and maybe doggie paddled the rest of the way—something I seriously considered. Anyway, I got out of the cab, threw some money in the front window and got the heck out of there. That being said, the Cardinal Cruise was an absolute ton of fun....

I don't know if you've ever known any beer distributors, but they are very paranoid individuals. Until his passing three years ago, my brother was the largest beer distributor in the state of Iowa. He also was a huge Cubs fan. I don't know if it was a mix-up at the hospital or some sort of 4-H experiment that went haywire but, in fact, he was a Cubs season ticket holder. Back in the '70s, a lot of the jukeboxes in the Midwest, had not only "Here Comes the King—The Big Number One" song on them, but it also had, "When You've Said Budweiser, You've Said it All." From the time I was eight years old, in the summertime, I would listen to all the Cardinal games with Harry Caray and Jack Buck. I would hear those songs dozens and dozens and dozens of times during the summer. I loved those songs because it brought back wonderful memories of my childhood. What we love as a child we tend to cling to as an adult. Even though the Cardinals were actually a lousy team back then, **HARRY CARAY*** and Jack Buck just made the game so exciting, it was wonderful. Some years, during spring training broadcasts, I felt that the Cards had a chance to go 154-0. My brother would get so upset about the jukeboxes…he thought I was doing it on purpose because he was a Cubs fan. He never listened to any Cardinal games so he had no idea why I did that.

"The seventh inning retch" at Wrigley field is fun—especially when Harry used to sing it. Far better than Wrigley is the middle of the eighth inning at Fenway Park when 40,000 tone-deaf people sing "Sweet Caroline" as loud as they can. But nothing can compare to the eighth inning at Busch Stadium when Ernie Hayes used to play "Here Comes the King. Here Comes the Big Number One". It particularly brings back memories of the **PLAY-OFF*** days, when the wagon gate in right field would open and out would come the Clydesdales with Gussie sitting on top of the wagon wearing his big red hat. Unless you're a Cardinals fan, you just can't appreciate what all that means. To this day, at Cardinal games, in the eighth inning I tell my friends, "Do not even try to talk to me while that song is being played."

But like I used to tell my brother, "the Cubs are the team of the future, and always will be."

*In 1949, Harry Caray's first wife Dorothy **DIVORCED** him. In 1979 Harry wrote her: "Dearest Dorothy, Enclosed is my 360th alimony check. How much longer is this _ _ _ _ going to continue?" Dorothy responded: "Dearest Harry, Til death do us part. Love, Dorothy." Harry paid monthly till he passed away in Palm Springs in 1998.

*In a 2002 home **PLAY-OFF** game against the Arizona Diamondbacks, the Cards were saddled with a 10 p.m. start. The next day, after a huge outcry from Cardinal fans, Commissioner Bud Selig said, "I told our people, no more 10 p.m. starts. This is the end of it." Three years later on October 8, 2005 the Cardinals hosted the San Diego Padres… with a 10 p.m. start.

THE CARDS ARE NUMBER ONE ON HIS SHIP LIST

BILL HAYS, M.D.

Dr. Bill Hays is the King of Cardinal Fans in Herrin, Illinois—about two hours east of Busch Stadium. Hays and his wife, Pam, have had their lives change for the better after each of their 16 Cardinal Cruises from Altair Travel in St. Louis.

I n the spring of '85, the Cardinals sent out a letter saying they had planned a Cardinal cruise for that fall. Pam and I had never been on a cruise. The very first night we walked on board, the first person we met was Dal Maxvill. He couldn't have been more friendly. They were having a cocktail party that night. Ozzie Smith, John Tudor, Danny Cox, Whitey Herzog and Willie McGee were there. Jack Buck and **MIKE SHANNON*** were there. These guys were fantastic! They were all very friendly—very open. A guy that I met later that night became my closest friend, Marty Hendin, the late Cardinal executive.

The very first night, my wife got seasick. Mary Lou Herzog got seasick, too, so Whitey and I wound up talking to each other the whole night because our wives were in our state rooms throwing up! The cruise was a lot of fun—great food and great

---

***MIKE SHANNON** played high school football with Dick Musial and a few years later, Major League baseball with Dick's father, Stan Musial. In 1963, Stan said: "When your teammates are your kid's playmates, it's time to retire."

entertainment. We got to know the players on a personal basis. The other side of the coin was that we were much closer to the guys' ages at the time.

The next year, Todd Worell went, Terry Pendleton, Mike LaValliere and Vince Coleman. We've been getting Christmas cards from some of these guys since then. The cruise has a great atmosphere, and everyone is really friendly. The Cardinals make a real effort to take players who are very open and friendly and willing to talk to fans. You really get to meet the guys—at least we did—one on one, as a person and not just a watching him as a player. We made some long-lasting friendships out of that.

The second Cardinal cruise I went on, I got to know Mike LaValliere and his wife, Judy, fairly well. One day, we went on a junket to a beach and I started talking to Mike about which eye was his dominant eye in hitting. Mike said, "I have no idea what you're talking about." I showed him how to determine which was his dominant eye. I said, "When you bat, you want to make sure that you see the ball with your dominant eye because you can track it better." Mike seemed to pay attention to that, but I didn't think anymore about it. That spring, he was traded to Pittsburgh and he became a **.290-.300 HITTER***. All I told him was to adjust the way he held his head two to five degrees and he'd be hitting with the dominant eye. I wish I would have told him that on the cruise the year before.

Catcher Tom Pagnozzi was another nice guy. During a cruise, I asked him if he'd do a baseball card show for the John A. Logan College baseball team. He asked me, "Where does the money go?" The money goes to pay for their spring baseball trip. Pags said, "Yeah, I'll come down." Normally, they send someone out to pick him up. He said, "No, I'll take care of all that myself." It's about 100 miles—two to two and a half hours away. The day

---

***The difference between .250 hitter and a .300 HITTER is one hit per week.**

comes—it's January—and there is ice and snow everywhere! Pags shows up at my house that morning. We had breakfast and went over to the card show. Pags signed autographs four hours, all day long, friendly and nice to all the folks. Because of the snow, though, it was a poor turnout. At the end of the show, the coach, Jerry Halstead, gives Pags a check. Pags turned around and handed the check to me and said, "No, use this on your spring trip." It was about five thousand bucks. How classy was that?

HEAR ME NOW
LISTEN TO ME LATER

HENRY "CHAPPIE" CHAPMAN

Chappie Chapman is a legend in Peoria, Illinois. For twenty-nine years he was a broadcaster for WTVP, the PBS station and WMBD radio. In recent years, he's been a financial advisor with Wells Fargo. In his spare time, he and his wife, Jan, travel the world.

In my neighborhood in Pekin, Illinois, there were a number of Cub fans and not very many Cardinal fans. I wound up listening to **JACK BRICKHOUSE***, the Cubs announcer, because he was a Peorian. He graduated from Manual High School in Peoria, then moved onto WGN in Chicago and became the voice of the Cubs many light years before Harry Caray. My father was very annoyed that I had become a Cub fan, especially in light of the fact that both my father and mother were born in St. Louis. My father was known as "Chappie" and I was known as "Chappie, Jr." in those days and my mother's name was Clementine. My father had said to my mother, "Clemmie, this will not fly. We're taking Chappie Jr. to a Cardinal game, and we are going to persuade him as best we can to become a Cardinals fan. After the ballgame, we'll go to *Stan Musial and Biggies* down on Chippewa Boulevard, and hopefully Stan will be there and will be able to autograph a ball or a photo of himself."

*For many years, **JACK BRICKHOUSE** was the TV announcer for both the Cubs and the White Sox. The teams would televise home games only....When WGN-TV debuted in 1948. the first voice heard was Jack Brickhouse's.

We booked the game in June of 1950—I was twelve years old at the time. Enos Slaughter hit a two-run home run off of Robin Roberts, the Cardinals beat the Phillies 3-1. After the game, we went to *Stan and Biggies Restaurant* and Stan gave me an autographed ball with my legal name on it. He wrote, "To Henry Chapman, Best Wishes, Stan Musial." As fate would have it, Stan also gave me a photograph of himself in his unusual crouched position. He signed that one for me as well. I was so impressed because he was such a quality individual.

We finished dinner, got the ball and photo and were driving back from St. Louis to Pekin. I was sitting in the back seat and I just said, "Dad, I'm going to switch my allegiance from the Cubs to the Cardinals." He looked at my mother and said, "Clemmie, I knew it would work!" It has!

A couple of years ago, I had dinner with Mike Ditka at Mike's restaurant in Chicago. I happened to notice a huge painting hanging on the wall. It was a portrait of Stan Musial. I said to Mike, "I am so impressed that you have Stan's picture." Mike's response was, "Chappie, when I was a young lad growing up in Pittsburgh, I was looking for an athlete of Polish descent. I found 'The Man' ...Stanley Frank Musial, from nearby Donora, Pennsylvania. He became my boyhood hero. I used to lie in my bed every night and listen to Harry Caray on KMOX. Not only that, he's a quality guy. He comes to my restaurant whenever he's in Chicago.....which isn't that frequently anymore, because he's around ninety years of age and doesn't move around particularly well these days." It was a wonderful moment for both Mike and myself, to go back in time and talk about the boyhood hero that the two of us had in common...

Peoria is equidistant between St. Louis and Chicago, so we have a ton of Cub fans here but we have a ton of Cardinals fans here as well. I'm one of the owners of the Peoria Chiefs that up until seven years ago, was a Cardinal affiliate—the single-A franchise for the Cardinals. Walt Jocketty would come with his son, Joey, to our games on a periodic basis to see these young players and how they were developing.

I have a good friend, Don Fites, who I brought on to the board of the Chiefs. There are only four of us on the board. Don was on the board of the Tribune Companies in Chicago and is also the former Chairman and CEO of Caterpillar. He is a die-hard Cubs fan. One day Don said, "We have an opportunity to pick up the Class-A affiliation for the Cubs. The Cubs are more than willing to step up to the plate and do a lot of things for the ball club. I think it's to our advantage to embrace the Cubs."

So we made the switch...much to Walt Jocketty's unhappiness...but we did it and it's been a good franchise but I still wish that it was the Cardinals franchise. The Cardinals then moved to the Quad Cities and that's where the Cardinals Class-A Ball Club is...they're over in Davenport, Iowa.

That is until late 2012, when the Cubs took their affiliation to the West Chicago suburbs (Kane County) and we got the Cardinals back in **PEORIA***. Quad Cities is now a Houston affiliate.

*In late 1953 the Cardinals chose Jack Buck for play-by-play over Chick Hearn from **PEORIA**, Illinois. Buck got the job because he had done excellent Budweiser commercials that summer while broadcasting the Rochester Red Wings, the Cardinals' AAA team in New York. The Cardinals had just been purchased by Anheuser-Busch.

HE BOUGHT FAKE WORLD SERIES TICKETS THEN HE DRANK A SIX-PACK OF O'DOUL'S AND GOT INTO A FAKE FIGHT

PHIL HARDIN

Phil Hardin is a self-confessed St. Louis Cardinal junkie. He has amassed some amazing stories in his travels across this country to watch the Red- birds. Hardin lives in New Jersey, attended the Univer- sity of Dubuque on a football scholarship and his son turned out to be crazy about the Atlanta Braves.*

The year was 2004, and the Cardinals were in the World Series against Boston. As a die-hard Cardinal fan, the opportunity to see the Cardinals in a World Series game was a lifetime goal—obviously, you don't know when these things could happen again. Boston at the time had not won a World Series since 1918 so this was a very difficult ticket to get. I explained to my wife that the Cardinals are just up in Boston, which is a four hour ride. I could go, and if there was any way I could get a ticket, I would be able to see the Cardinals in the World Series without having to jump on an airplane and spend the night in a hotel. It was all relative!

I got the green light from her. On the Friday before the World Series started on that Saturday, I called my brother-in-law who lives in New Haven, CT. I asked if I could drive up after school and spend the night and cut the trip in half, I could drive to Boston the next morning. Well, when I got there, he decided he would like to go with me! On the way up, we put a sign on the car, "Wanted: World Series Tickets!" and added my cell phone number on the sign. We actually got three calls, and every caller wanted a thousand dollars a ticket, which is more money than I was going to spend. My brother-in-law, Matt, said that if we got only ticket that I was going to go in and he would watch it a sports bar.

We get to Boston pretty early and park at the Prudential Center. One of my friends told me that not many people realize it, but if you go to the concierge at different hotels, sometime people have given back their tickets and the concierge resells them. We tried a couple of hotels with no luck. One had just sold two tickets to the opening game. Again, mind you how much in demand this ticket was! We get on a Gray Line city tour bus and I put a sign on my Cardinal hat, "Wanted: World Series Tickets!" I had people chuckle at me saying, "Good luck! Who's going to sell a ticket to a Cardinal fan?" It made for good conversation. There were probably three or four more people who had tickets but wanted a thousand bucks for it...no way!

We ate at the Prudential Building, and we were walking to Fenway Park—a twenty minute walk. As we were walking, someone sees the sign on my hat and asks, "Do you need a ticket?" I responded, "Yes, we do!" He set a price at $800 per ticket. I thought, "No way." I knew, with scalpers, you never take the first price they ask. I told him I'd give him face value. He countered with another price, and finally I got it down to $300 per ticket. I shelled out $600 and told my brother-in-law, "This is your Christmas present!" We made our way and I was happy as can be! I was going to meet a lifetime goal of seeing the Cardinals play in a World Series!

When we got to Fenway, they scanned the tickets and we found out that we had bought bogus tickets! I couldn't believe how real they looked! I wanted to go back and get my money back, but my brother-in-law wisely talked me out of it! Why make a bad situation worse.

I was still determined to get into the game...this is a lifetime goal of mine! My emotions went from extremely high to really down in the dumps. I just lost $600. I still wanted to get inside and we're still pretty early. I'm holding up my fingers, and people are walking by and laughing at the Cardinal fan trying to get tickets in Boston. Most of it was in good fun and I enjoyed the bantering back and forth. I said to my brother-in-law, "Here's what has to happen. Somebody had to be coming to the game and at the last second couldn't make it, so they would just want to get rid of the ticket real quick so they wouldn't miss anything." We spread out, and sure enough, I found someone selling a ticket for $250 with face being $150. I showed the seller the fake tickets and asked if we could pay him once we were inside so we wouldn't get scammed again. He said, "No way! You know I could make a lot more than $250 for this ticket." He showed me three other tickets in the same section, different seats, so he convinced me they were legitimate. I gave a ticket to my brother-in-law and I said, "I have the section written down. When I get a ticket to get inside, I will find you, and if I don't see you and the end of the game comes, we'll meet at the **TED WILLIAMS*** statue."

Yawkey Way at Fenway Park is a closed off street when there is a game. As I was walking, there was a side door that was ajar. I felt that I could slip through there. Even if they noticed me, I could show them the fake ticket! I thought I could have made it. I started thinking though, I might get arrested.

I'm still looking for a ticket. The game starts, and there are still tickets out there on the street, but they are being sold for $1000. I won't pay that! Of course, now I'm real suspicious if any of those tickets were going to be legitimate or not. The game is

---

***TED WILLIAMS** and his son John Henry are among 161 frozen bodies world-wide awaiting a cryogenic rebirth...157 are stored in three U.S. facilities...The two Williams men are in Scottsdale, Arizona...In real life many are cold, but few are frozen.

going, and of course, I want to see the game. There was a sports bar there, so I went over where I could see the game on TV through the window. There was a maximum capacity of people that were allowed in the sports bar. Nobody could get in until somebody came out. There was a line of 25 people.

I would watch a half inning from outside looking in at the television. The Cardinals fell quite a ways behind pretty early. I would go at the half inning and walk around looking to find a ticket. I couldn't get a ticket and the next half inning would come so I would watch through the window again. About the third inning, I said, "You know! It's just not happening!" I walk to a Dunkin' Donuts. I just plopped myself down and I said to the employee, "Do you mind if I sit here for quite a while and watch the game? The other member of my party is in the game and we're going to connect afterwards." A policeman comes in and sits down rather close to me. He strikes up a conversation about the game. The Cardinals were coming back and it turned out to be a very exciting game. I had a gained a comfort level with this policeman. I said to him, "I want to tell you something. I bought these two tickets, and as real as they look, they are fake and we couldn't get in." I don't know what kind of response I was looking for, but he really didn't care. "That happens! You have to be careful!"

I thought about things, "What do I want to do?" One of my thoughts was that this could happen at tomorrow's game too, which was a Sunday. There was a newspaper there—the Boston Globe. I called and asked for the sports department, got through and said, "Listen. I just wanted to know if tomorrow you could print something in the paper—a little "buyer beware" that there are people selling fake tickets." They told me, "We're going to have one of our reporters call you back." I gave them my cell phone number and just waited. I never got a call for the rest of the night. When the game ended, I met my brother-in-law and we walked back to our car at the Prudential Building. At the time, they had a policy that if you present your ticket on the way out, they give you free parking. As we're pulling up to leave, the fake ticket got us free parking! It was an expensive way to get free parking but at least we got something! The next morning, I was driving from Connecticut back to Jersey and my phone rings. It is the Boston Globe. I said, "You guys are a little late—the Sunday papers are already out." Well, they asked me a whole bunch of questions: "Where do you live? How did you become a Cardinal fan? How much did you pay? What street corner? What did they look like?" I must have talked to them a half hour! They didn't fulfill my wishes though...I wanted something in the paper on Sunday to alert the fans.

I got home and went to work the next day. My wife and I are both teachers in the same school. I didn't want anybody to know about this so I told my wife not to let anyone know what happened. Well, my name got on the internet. When I went to school, there were a fair amount of people who already knew about it! Now the word had spread all over school, and I'm dealing with all kinds of questions. My wife called home, as she often did, to retrieve any phone messages, and there were six different news agencies out of Boston, all of which wanted me to call them back.

I start thinking, "This story is going to have a happy ending. Someone is going to feel sorry for me and they are going to give me tickets when the Series comes back to Boston for Game 6 or 7." I called whatever news agency it was. Unbeknownst to me, my name was on the front page. "Fake Tickets Sold, see page 3." I told them all the whole thing about the fake tickets. I was wondering why there was so much interest in them talking to me. My brother-in-law found out that The Mob was involved and that the police chief of Boston was holding a news conference. An arrest had been made, but others got away.

Well, we were at the supper table, and the phone rings. It's another Boston news agency. They say to me, "We'd like to come to your home and interview you tonight." I'm thinking,

"You're going to drive four hours from Boston to my house to interview me tonight? That doesn't make any sense!" They told me they had a stringer—someone who works for the newspaper but lives in a different state. They said that person could be to my house in a hour. I said, "That's fine, but the directions to my house are very difficult." Now, that was 2004, and I wasn't very familiar with GPS yet. They just wanted the address with no directions. "As long as we have the address, we'll be there!"

I called my brother-in-law back and said, "You won't believe this! Now they are coming to our house to interview me!" All the time I am still thinking something good is going to come out of this story and I'm going to get tickets to Game 6 and Game 7. My brother-in-law says to me, "How do you know it's not The Mob coming to your house! The Mob is involved in the selling of these tickets!" He has me thinking! "Where is this going?" My wife's a little worried.

I get a phone call from the person that is coming to my house. He said, "Very funny! You gave me a bogus address!" I said, "Look! I told the person on the other end that our house is very hard to find, and I tried to give him directions and they refused. Where are you?" He said, "There is no such address as what you gave us in Verona, New Jersey!" I told him, "I didn't say Verona...I live in the town of Vernon." These towns are 45 minutes apart. The man said, "I don't have time to drive to your house, and then drive back down here and get the story to Boston before the 11:00 news and they want your story on the 11:00 news." He asked me if I could meet him at a diner a little more than half way. I agreed. I purposely did not wear anything that had "St. Louis Cardinals" on it, which it's hard for me to put something on that *doesn't* have "St. Louis Cardinals" on it. They have no idea what I look like. I get there and sure enough, there is a person outside in the parking lot. They have lights all set up and are just waiting for me to arrive. I watched them a little bit from the distance. There was a man and a lady that seemed very legitimate. I went up to them and introduced myself, not knowing what to expect. Again, I was thinking of the silver lining at the end of this story. I ended up telling them the whole story. They interviewed me for 15 minutes and then I went home. I got a phone call the very next day from a friend of mine in Vermont, "Phil, I was watching the television, and I stayed up to watch the sports. Holy cow! Your story came on!" It was neat that a friend of mine from Vermont got to see my story on television. Much to my disappointment and Cardinal fans disappointment, the series wrapped up in St. Louis in a four-game sweep, so even if there was anybody to feel sorry for me to give me tickets, it never came back to Boston.

THERE'S NO PROOF THAT SMOKING CAUSES CANCER... WELL...THERE'S NO LIVING PROOF

GREG HOWARD

Greg Howard left small town life in Illinois when he crossed the big bridge to St. Louis 13 years ago. For the last 10 years, he has been part of the A Team at America Sports Bar and Grill located inside Ameristar Casino in Saint Charles, MO. At the age of seven, he became hooked because of his fascination that Keith Hernandez hit a home run on his birthday during the '82 World Series. He presently calls Hillsboro, MO home where he and his wife raise their two children.

Back around 2001, Southwest Airlines was running a deal for $39 each way from Lambert Airport to Chicago Midway. We didn't have tickets for the Cubs-Cardinals series, but we grabbed the cheap airfare and flew up there. We booked a cheap hotel and we were all shacking up together to save money...there were four of us in a room. On the day of the game, we waited until the second inning...we just sat in the Cubby Bear Tavern and had us a few beers because we couldn't find seats. The scalpers down on the street were really trying to stick it us. After the second inning, we went outside **WRIGLEY***

*In 2005, Jimmy Buffett had the first two concerts ever held at **WRIGLEY** Field. Buffett dedicated, "Take Me Out To The Ball Game" to Harry Caray, calling Harry "an old pirate." Buffett has also performed at Fenway Park and five other big league stadiums since that initial performance at Wrigley.

and found a guy who actually ended up selling us tickets for a little cheaper than face value.

After the game, we walked out of the gate right where the Cardinals bus always pulls up. They always try to angle the bus to block people from getting in and out, and they put barricades around the back side of the bus so people can't get in and mess with players when they're loading up.

The girls with us had to use the restroom, so my buddy and I were standing out in front of Wrigley Field in front of the bus. There were literally thousands of people streaming out of Wrigley at the time. I was standing there smoking a cigarette and T.J. Matthews, who was a relief pitcher for us back then, was climbing on the bus. I don't think he played that day, so he probably didn't shower and beat everyone onto the bus.

There are people all around us, and we notice T.J. Matthews tapping on the bus window. We look up at him and he starts pointing to us, and he's making a gesture with his finger. Basically, he was asking my buddy for a cigarette. We had no idea if he was talking to us or if he was trying to get one of his friends' attention or if maybe he knew someone else out there. We looked around and then looked back at the bus, and he shakes his head and mouths "No!" and then he points at us and says, "No!...you guys...you got another cigarette?" I held up the pack of smokes and said, "Yeah, I've got some!" Matthews gestures for us to come around to the back of the bus.

When we walk around to the back of the bus, we see the emergency door open up and he jumps off and pulls the barricades to the side. "Come on in here". So we walked up and give him a cigarette and he's standing outside smoking a cigarette with us waiting for the rest of the team to get there. Then he asks us what we're doing in town and if we were having fun. Then he asks, "What are you guys doing tonight?" We say, "Well...nothing...we're just going take in the town and party a little bit." He says, "Well, if you want, come down and hang out with me and some of the players at the Westin Hotel. You guys can't dress in your Cardinals clothes, though. Do you have some nice clothes that are not Cardinals attire? We don't want to draw too much attention." We said, "Yeah, yeah, we've got some nice stuff!" He said, "Alright, well come on down to the Westin about 7 o'clock. We'll have a couple of drinks and just hang out."

We walk back around to the side of the bus and find the girls to let them know what just happened! We tell them "Hey! T.J. Matthews just invited us out on the town tonight. He wants to hang out! He wants us to meet him at the Westin at 7:00." At first they didn't believe us. "We swear he just invited us, except he told us we have to dress nice. We can't wear Cardinals stuff." The girl said, "Well, we didn't bring anything nice. All we brought was Cardinal gear and shorts. What are we going to do?" I suggested, "Let's go down to Michigan Avenue and we'll do a little shopping...kill a little time...buy some new clothes...then go back to the hotel...get cleaned up and go out!"

That's what we did! We went down to Michigan Avenue, which by the way, there's nothing there that's cheap. We all bought brand new pants, shoes, shirts and belts. We literally had nothing with us except tennis shoes, shorts and Cardinal jerseys. We went back to the hotel, got cleaned up, and took a cab to the Westin Hotel.

We got to the hotel a little early, about 6:30, so we ordered a drink. We sat at the bar and started drinking. The Westin is not cheap either...the drinks ran about $7.00 -$7.50 each, not including a tip! We were sitting at the bar having a drink and 7 o'clock rolls around. We're not seeing T.J. Matthews anywhere. We were thinking he was just running late, so we were ordering drink after drink.

The night rolls on and 7 o'clock turns into and 8 o'clock. 8 o'clock turns into 9 o'clock, and 9 o'clock turns into 10 o'clock. We were talking the whole time, "Hey! I think someone's playing us!" By this time, the girls really don't believe that we even met T.J. Matthews, "You guys are just putting us on!"

I realized the next day was Sunday and remembered they had a day game, so I said, "Guys, the players have a curfew. If we haven't seen them by now, we're not going to see them at all. They're not coming down, so we might as well just pay our tab and get out of here." We got our tab from the bartender and it was ridiculous! I thought we broke a window. I don't remember exactly, but it was very expensive at $7.50 a drink. The tab was at least $200- $300 before the tip. We paid the bartender and as we're leaving I say to the bartender, "Just out of curiosity, we were invited down here by one of the Cardinal players. We were supposed to meet him here at 7 o'clock and we never saw him. Have you seen any of the players in the lobby or anywhere?" The bartender starts laughing and he said, "I wondered why you guys were hanging out for so long?" Then he says, "Man, they don't stay at this Westin, they stay at the Westin down the street! You're at the wrong one!" We were all in shock, and by that time it was too late to meet up. We knew they would no longer be there. I can't believe we missed our chance to hang out and maybe even meet a lot of the Cardinals that night and have a good time. At least we got a good story out of it! We ended up staying for the Sunday game, we got some scalped tickets and went to the game. We were all pretty hung-over that next day.

SO SAY YOU ONE
SO SAY YOU ALL

Rogers Hornsby, who had a .358 lifetime batting average, not only holds the highest single-season batting average in Cardinals history, amazingly he holds the same record for the Cubs and the Braves! Hornsby was known as an irascible SOB as a manager and as a player. He's buried in Hornsby Bend, Texas, which isn't on any real map of any consequence. To get to his grave site, I had to go down a dirt lane past a "No Trespassing" sign. There was a barbed-wire fence along each side of the lane. After walking for a little while there was a historic marker there relating about Ruben and Sarah Hornsby, who had built a home at that spot in 1832. It said that "the house was known for its Christian hospitality," but it was also the place where Josiah Wilbarger recovered after being scalped in 1833. Finally, I got to the burial area, which was full of tombstones for the Hornsbys. Rogers' grave was way over in the back corner, covered by plants and underbrush and grass. There was no one else buried near him. He died in 1963 at the age of sixty-seven....

Babe Ruth's grave is in Hawthorne, New York, at the Gate of Heaven cemetery. Also buried at the same cemetery are Jimmy Cagney, **BILLY MARTIN***, Westbrook Pegler, and Sal Mineo. Ruth's grave was considerably more gaudy than Lou Gehrig's—which is only 5 miles away. Ruth's had American flags planted nearby. It had a big picture of Jesus with a little boy, a little Babe Ruth, and it had inscriptions on each side of that picture of Jesus. More than ten people a day visit the grave, and most of

*In 1974 **BILLY MARTIN** was managing the Texas Rangers and Frank Lucchesi was his third base coach. Martin tried using a transistor hook-up to his coaches to relay signals. One game the system was broken, but Martin kept yelling instructions for a suicide squeeze into the microphone. Red Sox pitcher Luis Tiant finally stepped off the mound and yelled: "Frank, Billy said he wants the suicide squeeze."

them leave different things. When I was there, there were four baseballs, a Louisville Slugger bat with a crack in it, a Baby Ruth candy bar, four American flags, fifty-one cents in change, and notes from a half-dozen different people.

—**Dave D'Antonio**, Santa Clara, CA

A few years ago while traveling past Donora, Pennsylvania on the Pennsylvania Turnpike, my wife suggested to me that maybe we should take a side trip to see where Stan Musial lived as youth. We located the house where he grew up. Across the street from his boyhood home, on the front porch, sat a man that I judged to be a little older than myself. I approached this gentleman and 45 minutes later left the premises with a big smile on my face. The man was a boyhood friend of Musial and he'd spent sleepovers with Stan in their youth. He talked at length about Stan's ability to shoot marbles. I had always thought that Pee Wee Reese was the big league marble champ. I didn't realize the many other talents of my hero—shooting marbles being one—playing the harmonica being another...I do have a Musial harmonica.

—**Charles "Bud" Berge**, Allentown, PA

Chapter Four

A FEMALE CARDINAL FAN

No Man Is Worthy

WHEN MLB CALLS
YA GOTTA ACCEPT THE CHARGES

LAURA JANASKE

Laura Janaske is a Washington County dispatcher in Nashville, IL. You may recognize her from MLB's "I Live For This!" commercials. When she's not in the "Sea of Red", you may be able to find her collecting awards at the Washington County Fair for her cross-stitched creations.

My grandfather is the one who introduced me to the game of baseball, however, it was my dad who took me to my first game at Busch Stadium. I'll never forget it because it was Kids Jersey Day which is really just a t-shirt. Thank God it was, because it was about 120 degrees down in the field box and our seats were in the sun. My dad kept taking my shirt to the bathroom, soaking it in cold water and putting on my head to keep me cool. I'll never forget that day!

A lot of people may remember MLB's "I Live For This" Campaign from 2005. Major League Baseball Promotions were looking for the biggest fan or the fan that the producers thought would best reflect their actual cities. I entered an on-line contest and won a "front-of-the-line" pass. I didn't want to take off work because it takes an hour for me to drive down to the Stadium, but since I won the pass, I knew I had to go. I was thinking, "What do I wear? What do I say? What do I do?" When I got there, I did just like they told us to do…"just come like you would to the game."

I didn't go overboard. I just talked about all of the stories with my grandpa. I also told them about going with my sister and crying during Opening Day. I made it through the first cut, and then I had to go in front of the directors. That was amazing! When I received a call back from Matthew Leach with MLB I just about jumped out of my shoes.

A week went by and I had not heard anything more from them. Then, the very first day that I was back at work, the phone rang and it was MLB calling to tell me that I was one of three finalists! I nearly passed out! After another round of interviews, I waited all weekend long and then they called me on Monday to tell me that they had selected me...Laura Janaske...to represent the St. Louis Cardinals in the "I Live For This" Campaign.

Over the week of February 14, 2005, they flew me first class to Miami to film with the Oscar winning director Peter Gabriel, who had previously directed the documentary, *Hoop Dreams.* We filmed six hours of footage. It was basically back and forth bantering, similar to the interview process. They asked questions about my experiences with baseball and my opinions about various topics.

One of the funny quirks about the commercial was when I said, "Howdy!" I thought that we were on a break! I didn't realize that the cameras were still rolling. I heard somebody saying,. "Well, I'm a Texas fan" I just made a little joke and said, "Howdy!" and that's the part they kept! We did six hours of filming for a thirty-second spot. It aired for three months, and they even paid me royalties. It was a nice experience and I was really honored to do it. Honestly, I would have done it for free!

When they were doing the interview process, I wanted to do something that they would remember me by. At the time, I was working for Anheuser-Busch and had a bunch of red sunglasses. I wrote "STL" on each pair of the sunglasses....my calling card.

When I walked into the room with all of the producers, directors, bright lights and cameras...for most people it would have been overwhelming...however, I took it as an opportunity. I was wearing my sunglasses and said, "Welcome to St. Louis and to Cardinal Nation. I SEE that you don't have any red on? I would like you to SEE baseball like I do!" I then gave each one of them a set of the sunglasses that I had made with the "STL" logo on them. I said, "I don't just SEE Cardinal Red, I swim in the SEA of Cardinal Red!" Between that play on words and the interview process, we came up with a couple of different versions of it and that's how it ended up in the commercial.

I won't lie to you....I came to Opening Day that year wanting to be recognized from my commercial and it didn't take long! When I got off the Metrolink, I signed autographs, held babies and took pictures with people. There was a group of four retired ladies who wore *Cat in the Hat* style hats to the game that said, "Let's go Cards!" They also wore homemade Cardinal shirts. I autographed the bags that they were carrying. Now they look for me every year. We always do a photo every year...

When I went down to the Stadium for Game 1 of the 2011 World Series, I didn't have a ticket. I tried to get one through the scalpers, but they were way too high. I ended up hanging out in the parking garage at Stadium East with Cornbread, a local radio station personality. We watched the first few innings of the game from up there. Around the third inning, I told Cornbread that I was going over to Paddy O's to get something to eat and use their bathroom and that I would be back.

When I was walking around the perimeter of the Stadium to get over to Paddy O's, I found a piece of paper on the ground, I picked it up, turned it over, and it was a ticket!

I took it up to the gate guy and I said, "Sir, I found this on the ground. Can you scan this and tell me if it's good?" He scanned it and said, "Well it's not really working, go check at the ticket window." I checked with the guys at the ticket window and they told me, "It's a StubHub ticket, it's not good." I went from feeling way high to feeling way low and kicking rocks as I headed to Paddy O's. When I got to Paddy O's, they had put all of the food away already, so by then I'm really kicking rocks!

On my way back to the parking garage, I found another ticket! It felt like the movie, *Charlie and the Chocolate Factory,* where Charlie finds the money in the sewer, buys a candy bar, and finds The Golden Ticket. I couldn't go back to the same gate guy because the usher would think that I was just pulling these out of thin air. I went to the next gate, and the lady there looked like she was crabby—just really having a bad day. I then found this really sweet looking grandpa guy at the gate on the first base side. I gave him the same story and handed him the ticket. He scanned it and it made the normal "bling" noise, as it does for a valid ticket. I went running full blast into the Stadium before he could change his mind!

My night did not end there. I went into the game in the fourth or inning. The Cardinals ended up winning. I then found a program, unharmed in a bag. It was a $30.00 World Series program that someone had left behind. I got great pictures and autographs during the entire day. I decided that I must be having some good luck, so I stopped by a casino on my way home.

When I walked into the casino there was a machine with 11 credits remaining on it! I thought, "Now this is a sign!" I put my twenty dollar bill into the machine and won $150.00! I said, "That's it! I'm done!" However, I did buy a lottery ticket on the way home, but that was the end of my luck for that night. That day was so cool!

FEMALE CARDINAL FANS ARE SOME OF LIFE'S MOST MISUNDERSTOOD CREATURES

SUE TRETTER

Sue Tretter began her studies of the Cardinals and baseball when she was a little girl sitting on her father's lap. She now has a PhD in American Studies and has taught at Lindenwood University since 1994. Before that, Tretter taught at St. Louis University. Getting ready to retire, Tretter will pursue one of her dreams of writing a book that incorporates her love for the game. She and her husband live in Maryland Heights, MO.

D ad always worked in a machine shop and after work, he'd have dinner, sit down with his Budweiser, and turn on the ballgame. I know that we listened to quite a few ballgames on the radio but, as far back as I can remember, we had television. When we went to my grandmother's house...it was a three room house in South St. Louis...it was just packed. She had five kids and they had kids and they had kids! I don't know how the house stood it! We would all be huddled in the kitchen...standing room only...listening to the ballgames. Everybody had to hush up!

Then, we would have family barbecues and the men would go out back to the alley and play baseball with bottle caps! When I tell my students about that...first of all they want to know where did you get the bottle caps! Well, there are some bottles that now have bottle caps. I remember going to see Daddy play cork ball too. There were nets around the field—like a cork ball Stadium. He just loved sports! Every night when he sat down, I was there on his lap and I was watching. I had two brothers— the oldest was interested in soccer and the youngest was interested in **NASCAR***. I was the only one who was interested in baseball. It was a disappointment to dad and to me to find out that I really could not play baseball.

My Daddy ended up working at Anheuser-Busch. He was a stockholder and they would have stockholder meetings. Some of the Cardinals would come. The stockholders always got two pairs of tickets to two different games. Otherwise, my parents rarely went to the games. My father was never one for crowds. At a game, when people in his aisle would get up from their seats to go somewhere, it would just ruin his whole day....

I'm so glad the Cardinals returned to KMOX. I grew up with KMOX...it wasn't the Cardinal game my dad listened to. He listened to Bob Hardy and Jim White. They'd always talk about St. Louis things too. They would get on air and say, "Oh! Go to Dohacks if you want some good coconut cream pie—it's the best in the world!" It is sad that all these places are gone. Back at that time, there was so much going on in the city. On the way home from my grandmother's house we would go to Sam The Watermelon Man. He had these big tubs that had ice in them so the watermelons would be ice cold. We'd go in the back yard and sit at the picnic table and light flares to keep bugs away. It was a neat, simple time back then. I remember **STAN AND BIG-GIES***—they had such great food!

Getting back to the class, we look at what is culture and then how is baseball a culture. Well, a culture has its own food. Baseball has its own food...peanuts, popcorn, Crackerjack. It

---

*In 2011, Forbes named Dale Earnhardt, Jr. the "Most Valuable Athlete Brand"—higher than any NFL or Major League player...only four **NASCAR** drivers are from southern states...Danica Patrick has appeared in more Super Bowl commercials than any other celebrity with ten.

***STAN MUSIAL AND BIGGIE'S**, the famous restaurant in the '60s and '70s, was located at 5130 Oakland. The top entrée cost $10.50.

has its own music. There are so many baseball songs written—people have no idea how many songs have been written. It has its own literature and its own language. It has its rituals. In fact, Yankee Stadium was known as the **HOUSE THAT RUTH BUILT***. People refer to the Hall of Fame as a Cathedral. If you look at people during a game, they almost look as if they are praying. They have their hands together over their mouths—I don't necessarily think they are praying but they're in that position! Then you have the rally caps and The Wave. In fact, I have my students do The Wave in class. There are a lot of foreign students in there, and they don't know what it is. I ask them, "Do you want to know what that is?" and they say, "Yes." "They are all adoring their professor!" Then I tell them the truth.

I show the kids various souvenirs that people collect. Do you know that if you wanted, you can get a baseball Cardinal coffin, or if you're cremated you can get a Cardinal urn? What a way to go out! Actually, we buried my dad with his Cardinals' hat on. He had all his Marine pins but had his Cardinal hat on...it just made sense...

When So Taguchi came, my father just loved him. Every time he came into the game, he would say, "There's So Taguchi!" It always baffled me. I thought, "So, So is your favorite player right now and when you were younger, you were over in his country fighting." My father really never did have any racial hatred or anything against the **JAPANESE*** people. He told me it was the most beautiful country he had ever seen, and he

*Babe Ruth attended St. Mary's School in Baltimore. St. Mary's is now called Cardinal Gibbons High School and is known as **THE HOUSE THAT BUILT RUTH**.

*The Yomiuri Giants are sometimes called "The New York Yankees of **JAPAN**." They have won the most pennants and have the deepest fan base in Yakyu (Japanese Baseball)....The Nippon Ham Fighters give free tickets to foreigners on "Yankees Day."

wished he could go back one more time. He never did make it back but we have pictures of him when he was on Okinawa playing baseball with the kids. Maybe So Taguchi's father learned baseball from one of the GIs!...

My husband and I went to Boston and we sat down...the seats are so small. I said, "We have seats like this in St. Louis!" He said, "Where?" and I said, "In the history museum!" One of the guys from Boston leaned over with this Boston accent, "Lady, we don't put our stuff in museums...we use it! Fenway *is* a museum!"...

I did a class on Emerson and the Transcendentalists and we were looking at various aspects of the American life that were transcendental. At the time of our class, there was a baseball game just starting. We decided that we would go that day, so we all went down to the ballpark. I told them they each had to write a two-page paper on what they found to be transcendental at the ballpark. I've never had such thoughtful papers from a group of students, and it wasn't just BS. They truly found a sense of serenity and a shared spirit at the ball game. Everybody is your friend at a ball game. You are high-fiving everyone! There is a shared spirit when we're there at the ballpark.

MARRIAGES ARE MADE IN HEAVEN, SO ARE THUNDER AND LIGHTNING

ELIZABETH HELLER

Elizabeth Heller, a native of Belleville, has been a Mallinckrodt employee for 11 years and a die-hard Redbird fan for three times that number.

In 2003, it finally happened—my boyfriend proposed and I was going to get married! I have dreamed about being a fall bride for most of my life, and was just so happy that my waiting for Mr. Right paid off. My now fiancé was excited because he had always told me that the year he gets married, the Cardinals would win the World Series, so to him 2004 was going to be a good year!

As I got into wedding mode, my first priority was booking the church and the reception hall for an October date—my favorite month of the year. I never imagined how difficult that was going to be. First of all, finding a date that the church and the venue both had open was hard enough, but adding my fiancé into the equation made it a task! I found a date...Oct 2...so I asked if that would be good for him. His response was, "That's the end of baseball season. The Cardinals *could* be in the wild card race, we can't do it then."

A bit annoyed, I obliged because I know how much he loves his Cardinals. I called the church and our reception venue and canceled that date and booked Oct 9. I went back to him and told him the good news. He responded without hesitation, "Well...that would be the Divisional Playoffs. We can't get married during the Divisional Playoffs." By this time, I'm getting a little frustrated because my dream of an October wedding seemed like it was fading. I checked more dates and they had the 16th and the 30th left but someone was a maybe on the 30th.

I thought I was smart this time and talked to him before booking the dates. With regards to the 16th, he said, "There's no way! That would be the National League Championship Series!" I, probably not so nicely, said, "How do you know they're going to be in the NLCS?" Even though I thought he was doing it for himself, he did bring up a good point. "I just don't want it to be the same night if it is—people may not show up to our wedding because they will have playoff tickets. I just don't want you to get your feelings hurt."

Well, I was dead set on doing this in October so the 30th it was. There was no option at this point. He said, "Fine...October 30th. If we're going to do October 30th, that is going to be during the World Series. Make sure that it's the day that the National League is on the road so people will be less likely to miss the wedding to go to the World Series." I didn't really have that option, so I booked it...October 30th, 2004.

Well, I was getting nervous the closer the wedding got. Although the month leading up to the wedding was fun and exciting celebrating all the Cardinal victories, it also meant that Game 6 of the World Series would be the same night as our wedding. I started calling around to see how much a big screen TV would be to bring to the reception so if people were watching the game, at least they could be in with the party! As you know, we didn't need to rent that TV...the Cardinals were swept by Boston in an historical victory for the **RED SOX*** and our wedding turned out to be the most beautiful day ever!

In 1944, Franklin Delano Roosevelt's last campaign speech ever was at **FENWAY PARK...*

When my daughter was three, it seemed to be the year of the Cardinals in our household. Livvy loved watching games with her daddy and knew players, past and present, by number. April came and the start of the 2011 season. A week after the Good Friday tornadoes swept through St. Louis, I took my daughter to the Bridgeton library, and I noticed the Secret Service mulling about. I hadn't heard anything in the news, but thought maybe some politician was coming to look at the extensive damage our town suffered during the storms. Well, it turned out that former First Lady Laura Bush was in town to dedicate a teen center in the library. It was unannounced because they didn't really want any media there. They didn't want to bring attention away from the devastation of the tornado. Channel 5 was there only to document it for her.

We watched Laura Bush make her presentation at the teen center. She posed for pictures with different police officers and fire department personnel who were recognized that day. Before she left, she asked, "Does anyone else want a picture?" I was holding my daughter and said, "She would like to shake your hand." Mrs. Bush walked over and said to her, "Hi! What's your name?" She replied, "Livvy." She asked , "How old are you Livvy?" She said, "Three." She then asked her, "Do you like books?" Livvy nodded her head, "Yes." I said to Livvy, "Tell her what else you like." We had just checked out three books and three movies, so I was thinking she was going to say "movies" or "dvds" but she leaned forward to Mrs. Bush and whispered, "Baseball." Laura looked at her and asked me, "Did she just say baseball?" I just laughed and said, "Yes. She said baseball. She's whispering because she's in the library." Laura said to her, "Well Livvy, we like baseball too! We like the Texas Rangers." It was fascinating watching my three year old have a conversation with the former First Lady about baseball!...

In May, my mother-in-law came over to our house for a Mother's Day/birthday celebration. She brought over beautiful flowers to put in our garden and surprised our daughter with a gift too. Tish, my mother-in-law, found a baby turtle on her driveway at home and brought him to our house to have a loving home. Of course, we couldn't refuse, so we went to the pet store and made him a home.

That night we went to the Cardinal game. After the game, Yadi tossed a baseball to Livvy over the dugout as he walked off the field, so she decided that she was going to name her turtle Yadi. If you ask her why she decided on Yadi, she'll say "Because Yadi is slow running around the bases."

A month later, we bought two fish. We suggested to Livvy to name one of the fish "Red Schoendienst" because the fish was red. The other fish was chubby, so I asked my husband, "Is there a chubby player who played for the Cardinals?" The only player that he could think of was "Honey Bear" Rayford. So we named the other fish "Honey Bear."

The year goes on and we were at a playoff game when the Cardinals were playing the Phillies. My daughter was sitting on my lap wearing her Cardinal hat and jersey. The cameraman was standing at the end of our aisle and focused in on her to be on the big screen in the Stadium. She's never known her first finger to be her index finger...it's always been her "Cardinal finger" so I told her, "Look! You're up on the big screen!" what does she do? She puts up her Cardinal finger...she's a natural!

For Game 1 of the World Series, we were able to get standing room only tickets for the three of us. We went to the festivities downtown a bit early all bundled up despite the chilly weather. We were walking in before the game and saw two tents outside left field. Under the tents Jack Clark and Mike Matheny were doing meet and greets. Jack Clark had a line of fifty or sixty people, and Mike Matheny had absolutely no one in his line. They were both standing in front of a backdrop of the Stadium and taking photos with people. We didn't see Matheny at first because he kept stepping down off the platform because nobody was in his line. It was so nice—they printed out the pictures for us right there with a border that said, "World Series 2011." After we received the print, my husband told me that he had a Sharpie with him and suggested we try to get it autographed. Matheny was more than happy to sign and even personalized it for Livvy with her name, his signature and a biblical reference. This was, of course, before he was introduced as the next Cardinal Manager.

So to summarize, my daughter got a ball from Yadi. She was on the video board at Busch Stadium, she was on tv on the Fourth of July, she met Mike Matheny, she spoke to a former First Lady about baseball and attended a World Series game all in the a season when the Cardinals won the Championship! She probably had more memories in one season than I have had my whole life! She may not remember all of them but we have the pictures and videos so the memories will be forever preserved.

WHEN WE WERE YOUNG
AND OUR WORLD WAS NEW

PAM WHEELIS-TEMPLE

Pam Wheelis-Temple played softball for Assumption High School in East St. Louis. Wheelis-Temple attended Harris Stowe University and is now an accounting clerk at HD Supply Waterworks and lives in Florissant, Missouri, where she enjoys her version of the Man Cave.

When I was young, we would always try to go when there was a giveaway, because whether the Cardinals would win or lose, I would always get a **SOUVENIR***. My dad would get me a pack of baseball cards every time we went to the game. They weren't that expensive back then. I have about a thousand now.

When they took me to the Cardinal game on my 17th birthday, it was Seat Cushion Night. It was a good night! All the fans ended up throwing their seat cushions out on the field. It looked like it was snowing. I stayed in my seat with my seat cushion because that was my souvenir—I was not going to throw it out on the field! My mother and sister always wanted to leave early and I would say, "No! You have to stay until the ninth inning." My dad said, "Yeah, you have to stay until the last ball is pitched; you never know what's going to happen!"

---

*A male Oakland A's fan won a $510,000 settlement for sex discrimination... he was not given a **SOUVENIR** hat handed out to women on Mother's Day in 2004...a good lawyer knows the law, a great lawyer knows the judge.

Sure enough, that night the Cardinals won in the bottom of the ninth. It was a great night, and I am so glad I kept that seat cushion. Years later, in 2006, my husband took me to a Cardinal game on Seat Cushion Night. It was an anniversary gift. He wanted to leave early and I said, "No! We'll hang in there and win!" I was right! We won! David Eckstein got the game winning hit. He touched first base and all of the seat cushions went back out on the field again...but I kept mine. I still have them both today; they're hanging up in my "Pam-Cave".

My Dad was a Cardinal fan too. He's the one who taught me how to keep score because usually on Saturday afternoons, he would be outside doing yard work, and when he came in he would say, "Okay, what happened?" I could tell him what happened by my box scores! Now I've passed keeping score onto my husband. He's a mathematician and he wanted to have something to keep his interest, since he was born mathematically inclined. I said, "Well, here...I'll show you how to keep score, and then it gives you something to do while we're watching the game." It works out just fine!

I call my basement my Pam-Cave, but the official name is "Comfy Temple Stadium." When we moved to our house, my husband said, "What do you want to do with the basement?" and I said, "Let me decorate it." Thankfully, he said, "Okay." Before they tore down the previous Busch Stadium, I took pictures of different things around the ballpark, and had them blown up to poster size. I wanted it to be like you were in the Stadium and when you looked up, you would feel like you were sitting in the stands. I've got pictures of the Cap Dance and the scoreboard when fans would sing *Take Me Out To the Ball Game*. There is also one of the old Stadium with the Arch in the background. It turned out nice. Before my husband's father passed, he built bleachers for me as a Christmas gift. We had custom cushions made for the seat cushions, so now we have six seats on risers. It looks like bleachers. Home plate is underneath our television and we have grass-green carpet. I wrapped the support pillar in our basement in yellow fabric so that it looks like the foul pole. It's topped off with a red base-ball glove chair. After the Cardinals won the World Series in 2006, they had the World Series trophy on display at one of the U.S. Cellular stores in Florissant. I was very excited to have my picture taken with it! I had the picture blown up to poster size and that is the picture that you see when you go down into my basement. You know how some ladies have their "lady of the house" picture...well, that's mine!...

I have always liked Ozzie Smith. When I was a teenager, there was a hardware store named Central Hardware that had a contest where you had to write an essay in one hundred words or less about your favorite Cardinal. I remember saying

"Fredbird...**THE MASCOT***...because he never got traded." I won! I won a hundred tickets—I couldn't find that many people to go to the ball game with me! That was somewhere in the early 80s. It was a Sunday game and we ended up giving out tickets to the people in my church.

The Cardinals have had this promotion for the past couple years where Mobil On the Run gas station discounts their drinks when the Cardinals get six runs. You can get any drink, any size, for 50 cents. My four-year-old son looks at the television and says, "Did they get six yet?" At least, if nothing else, he knows how to count to six now! We adopted our son in 2008, and one of the first things we did was to take him to the ball game. We also went on Father's Day a couple of years ago, and we were down close to the Oakland A's dugout. My little boy had a green Cardinal hat on backwards. At the end of each inning, baseball players sometimes toss a ball into the stands for the fans. Well, one of the Oakland players had given the ball up to the one Oakland fan near the dugout. He turned around to give it to a little kid and saw that my son had a green cap on. It was on backwards so he looked like an Oakland A's fan, so he handed the baseball over to my son. The crowd behind us all said, "Awww." So then I turned my son's cap around and then the fans behind us yelled, "Yeah!" The A's fan turned around and saw that it was a Cardinals cap after all, and he said, "Uhhhh?" That's the first official Major League baseball that we have down in the cave.

My favorite Cardinal item that I have right now is my license plate. I was one of the first people to get a Cardinals license plate. It says "RDBDFN" (Red Bird Fan).

*The San Diego Chicken was once named by *The Sporting News* as one of the top 100 people in sports. He was never the official **MASCOT** of the San Diego Padres even though he got his start there. The Chicken in his heyday, would gross over $2,000,000 per year.... The only four Major League teams that do not have mascots are the Yankees, Angels, Cubs and Dodgers.

HE'S NOT HEAVY, HE'S MY BROTHER

SHEILA KOELLING

Sheila Koelling of Morrison, Missouri is the Catering and Special Event Coordinator for the Hermann Wurst Haus in downtown Hermann, Missouri.

In 1977, my parents had season tickets. One game out of the whole year we kids would get to go. We were one row back from first base, right on the first base line. Keith Hernandez was the first baseman. One game he handed me a foul ball that he had just caught. I looked at my Mom and asked her," Can I have it? Can I take this ball from this guy.?" He was a stranger to me, because I was only six at the time. She said, "Yeah, you can have it." Then Keith said, "Hey, ask your Mom if she has a marker or pen?" He signed that ball for me!

At that age, I didn't realize who Keith Hernandez was so the whole ball thing was not a big deal to me. I just thought, "Oh, a baseball." They were actually going in to bat when he stopped and leaned up over the fence and handed me the ball. They don't do that anymore. The players don't have a connection with the fans like they used to. Then, to stop and wait for a pen or Sharpie to sign the ball—that just doesn't happen either. I had my four brothers sitting next to me and I was the only girl. That was an easy choice for Hernandez, "Good, I don't have to pick which one of the boys to give the ball to. I'll just take the easy way out and give it to this little girl who's sitting here." That was in the second inning and every inning he waved to us kids. I thought, "So, who is this guy?" The players are not bigger than life when you're six years old.

I graduated from high school when my little brother was five. I went to Mizzou, and was always taking him to Mizzou Tigers baseball games and basketball games. He was always asking if he could get someone's autograph, and he would even do that at the Cardinals games. We would stand in line forever to get autographs. I was thinking, "Good grief! Are you kidding me?" However, since he was such a little guy and so much younger than the rest of us kids, we always just said, "Fine" and took him. We would say to each other, "I'll do it, but it's your turn next time."

Our grandfather had made a wooden base with a plexiglass case for that ball. One of the neighborhood kids kept saying, "It's a fake! It's a fake! That's not even real!" Well...I blackened his eye!

I used that autographed ball as a token to get my little brother to do his chores or to do his homework. I would tell him, "If you do your chores, I'll let you hold the ball" or "If you do your homework, I'll let you set it on your dresser for two days in your bedroom." That's why I gave it to him when he graduated from high school. I thought, "What else could I give this boy that my parents haven't already given him?" He had rebuilt a '64 Super Sport Impala and I had bought him personalized plates that said, "Sweet 64"...so I gave him those plates and the autographed ball for his graduation presents.

I don't know why he was so in to getting autographs. He was a weird kid about autographs, and he was always fascinated with that ball. I could get him to do just about anything by letting him hang out with that ball.

He always had to have his baseball hats or his t-shirts autographed. He wore this one Cardinals t-shirt until it was in rags. It had an autograph on it, and I wish I could remember whose autograph it was—I believe it may have been Ozzie Smith's.

It was always a huge joke in the family, because he had a Chicago Bears t-shirt and that St. Louis Cardinals t-shirt, and he would wear one every other day. Our mom kept saying, "My goodness, I'm going to wear these shirts out from just doing laundry!" This was when he was in high school and even then, he was not giving it up.

Four years after he got out of high school, he was killed in a car accident. When I went to clean my brother's house and pack up his things, I finally found that Keith Hernandez ball, which I still have. Now that ball is in the safety deposit box at the bank. I wish I had a picture of my brother with it. We buried him with the Cardinals shirt. I took his **CHICAGO BEARS*** shirt and wore it to bed for about year. Since I was so much older than he, we became very tight. It was like the older kids were raising the younger kids because mom and dad had to work.

We were raised in the country and we were poor, or what we considered to be poor. It was a huge privilege for us to go to one game a year. Our parents went to a lot games, but we didn't. We had chores and different things that we had to do. However, my little brother was a little more privileged than the rest of us. Mom and Dad spoiled him rotten. Maybe that's why all of that stuff was different for him, because he didn't have the responsibilities as a kid that we did. The autographs meant so much more to him and we felt like, "Eh, whatever!" I never realized what a big deal it was until now.

Everyone in our family is a baseball fanatic and always has been. We couldn't wait until the Cardinals went to Spring Training. For us it went...Thanksgiving, Christmas, then Spring Training. Everybody else in the world, their lives revolved around Thanksgiving, Christmas, Valentine's Day...and then the end of school. Our world was Spring Training, home games, playoffs and then the World Series!

*Politician Mitt Romney's full name is Willard Mitt Romney. Willard from J. W. Marriott's middle name...and Mitt from his relative Milton "Mitt" Romney, a former **CHICAGO BEARS** quarterback.

YADA, YADA, YADA

My goddaughter is probably going to be the number one Cardinal fan! Her family and my son and I went to certain Cardinal games where they had "Run the Bases for the Kids Club" members after the game. She was so little; she was only two. We talked my son, Jackson, into running the bases with her. He is seven years older than she is. She was a little nervous, and we kept telling Jackson, "You have to take care of her, she's your responsibility. Don't let go of her hand. Don't run, just walk her, but if she runs, just walk a little fast with her." We had to line up in the basement of Busch Stadium, and just wait for our turn. We were getting a bit anxious. We got to the front of the line. I told her, "Make sure that you touch every base!" She understood and shook her head.

The Cardinal ushers lined the kids up and they went on to the field. My son held onto her hand the entire time, and like we told her, she stopped at every base. She didn't touch them with her foot, she stopped and bent over and touched every base with her hand! Jackson stopped with her and waited while she touched the base and then they walked on to the next base. The two of them could not have been smiling any bigger and she was just giggling! They came walking around third base and when she got to home plate, she tripped over the carpet... but she was having the best time! She just giggled and laughed. I'll never forget that day—just the two of them together and how good he was with her.

—**Brenda Pepper**, St. Charles, MO; Native of Virden, IL; Underwriter for AAA Insurance

My husband and I went to the Cardinal game with our kids. There were two guys behind us that started singing, "Yadi, Yadi, Hey! Yadi, Yadi, Yo!!!" We were laughing so hard because every time Yadi would get up to bat, they would sing that. Every time he would miss, they would sing really loud, "Yadi, Yadi, Nooooo!" All of the people were laughing, and the usher that was working the field kept turning around and looking at them, because they were so loud! Everybody was turning around looking at them! My kids were laughing, saying, "These two guys are crazy!"...

My oldest brother, Jim, is deaf—he's been deaf since he was two weeks old. He has always loved the Cardinals... watched baseball religiously...loved the game...and loved Orlando Cepeda. Orlando was, by far, his favorite player! There are six kids in my family. My mom would always say to my deaf brother, "You can't learn sign language. You need to be able to talk to people because it's a hearing world." That is why his speech is really pretty good! One night, he saw and talked to Orlando Cepeda for 15 minutes. After that, every time Cepeda would see him, he would tap my brother on the shoulder to make Jim look at him because Cepeda knew that Jim couldn't hear him if he said "Hey Jim, how ya doing?" At some games we would be sitting close and Cha-Cha would make it a point to acknowledge him in the stands. My brother was just crazy about him! At some point, I'm going to have to find him an Orlando Cepeda ball. Jim has autographed things from him when he was a kid, but I don't know if he can find them because they've been lost so many times.

—**Bridgette Velka**, Kay Jewelers, St. Louis, MO

When I was thirteen years old, I was a catcher for a girls softball team and I loved Tim McCarver more than anything in the whole world—I had a big crush on the man! The *Globe-Democrat* had announced they were having a baseball clinic and that Tim McCarver was going to be there to help out. It was being held on May 7, 1966 at Sportsman's Park, and it was one of the last events before the new park opened a few weeks later. However, at that time the clinic was for boys. It said, "Cardinal Boys Baseball Clinic." My nickname is "Arnie," so I submitted the request for tickets to the clinic under the name of "Arnie" for my friend and me.

When I received the tickets, my mother was concerned that we would not be able to get in once we got down there, so she called the newspaper and asked if they would allow us in. They begin putting an update in the paper stating that girls were also welcome. They also asked me if I would like to meet Tim McCarver, so of course, I was really excited!

We went to the clinic and Tim McCarver did not show up. I was really devastated. Instead of meeting Tim, I was able to meet catcher Pat Corrales, who was the nicest guy on earth. I have a picture of me with him signing my autograph book. It made the front of the *Globe-Democrat*'s sports page! After the event, my friend and I wrote him a letter and he responded. It was definitely a form letter, but it had personal information and they took the time to make sure that even though he didn't sign it, it was signed with his stamp. It contained specific information that we had talked to him about. I still have that letter and I also have the certificate from the clinic, which shows it was sponsored by the *Globe-Democrat* and KTVI. Out of 8,000 kids to show up, it was so neat that my picture made the front of the sports page! I also have the article that advertised the clinic and the update stating that girls were also allowed to come to the clinic. Sadly, Pat Corrales' wife died shortly thereafter while giving birth to their child.

St. Louis National Baseball Club, Inc.

June 1, 1966

Misses Maureen Guilfoy and
Jennifer Stockey
8528 Douglas Court
St. Louis, Missouri 63144

Dear Girls:

It took two of you to write, so we are going to see to it that it takes two of us to answer.

We certainly do appreciate having fans like you and, yet, Pat certainly does remember Maureen when she had her picture taken with him at the clinic.

You will have to excuse us for taking so long to answer your letter, but we have either been traveling or playing games since you wrote on May 7, and both of us are way behind in getting mail answered.

Since you wrote, though, things have changed with the Cardinals. You mention the 15-2 loss to the Giants and, let's face it, we are making every attempt possible to forget that loss.

Of course, a good thing happened the next day—we got Orlando Cepeda. And our club has certainly improved since we traded for him.

We think 1966 is going to be the start of many successful years for the Cardinals, and we certainly hope you will continue rooting for us.

Cordially,

Tim McCarver

Tim McCarver

and

Pat Corrales

Pat Corrales

TM/PC/lms

AUGUST A. BUSCH, JR., PRESIDENT / BUSCH MEMORIAL STADIUM / ST. LOUIS, MISSOURI 63102

Eventually, I did have my picture taken with Tim McCarver at one of the "Camera Days." I did get his autograph several times when he was coming out of the locker room after the games, however I never did get to actually talk with him.

My friends all teased me about McCarver not showing up. Of course, by that time, I didn't care that he had not shown up because I had decided that I loved Pat Corrales more. He was handsome and very charming and when you're thirteen years old, it doesn't take much to impress you.

I really don't follow baseball much anymore. Ever since they had the baseball strike, I just feel like it's not the same as it used to be when you would go out to the bleachers, pick out your own seat and bring your own beer.

—**Maureen Kylie**, Administrative Assistant at
JP Morgan-Chase, St. Louis, MO

I really have admired Red Schoendienst all the way from the beginning. In fact, I made a rosary for him from rose petals from the funeral of a Bishop from St. Louis whom he was very close to. I had one of the players give it to Red and I received a nice thank you letter back from him. He was very appreciative of me thinking to make him a rosary from those rose petals.

I have a sign on the back of my wheelchair that always draws a comment whether I'm at the games or not—"Cardinals" in bright sparkly color on a black background with "Number One Fan" underneath. I'm so proud of the Cards. In my window here, I have a big Cardinal on the Bat so that it can be seen from outside! I also have a Cardinals collection. I have shirts, jackets, and an ornament. The class who I was praying for at Sacred Heart Griffin High School sent me the Cardinal ornament for Christmas. It plays and lights up and is a real special part of my collection. Somebody else had given me a bottle of beer as a collector's item—one of those commemorative bottles. I have an umbrella too. I also have a picture of Fredbird with his beak on my head like he's trying to eat me!

When I was teaching in Bethalto, the kids were great fans. When I left there, they gave me a little bat that all of them had signed. I keep that with all of my Cardinal things. Let's see, I also have a light, it's probably about eight inches in diameter and in the shape of a Cardinals ball that can be used as a night light. I've got pins, necklaces, bracelets. I make Cardinal necklaces and bracelets, too! The Sisters get to enjoy my collection but I'm outnumbered here, 9-1; most of the other Sisters are Cub fans because they all come from the Chicago area. By rooting for the Cubs, I think they are repaying a debt to Satan. I'm know as *the* Cardinal fan here! Thankfully, there is at least one other. My driver, Sister Jean Patrick, is a Cardinals fan too! She manages to get to the games more often because she's able to get out more—plus she has the car!

If it's not too late, I'm hoping to get free tickets for my special friends—they call themselves "Special Friends". It's a group that I direct, a program for non-denominational persons with special needs in the Granite City area. I started down there with eight in '92 and I now have 56. The last two years we missed getting tickets because the Cardinals had run out of tickets for the dates that I put down. I just finished sending in again for tickets next year. One thing that I want to say about the Cardinals and persons with physical disabilities, I can't say enough about how I was treated personally at the old Stadium. I would be allowed to drive up to the VIP parking in front of this special ticket window. Someone would come to the car, take out my wheelchair and push me in. They would let us in at 6:00 and someone else would push me to my space. They would always find me a good spot. Everyone was great and they are still the most courteous and helpful people.

In closing, I will say...."GO CARDS!" I'll be watching!! I'm just not sure where.

—**Sister Mary Alice Mannix**,
Dominican nun in Springfield, IL

Mike Shannon's girlfriend, Lori, was doing a special charity event for the Special Olympics in **QUINCY, IL*** through her travel agency. Mike had told Ozzie what she was doing for the charity, so Ozzie grabbed two baseballs. He signed one of the baseballs and gave it to her and said, "Here, this is for your charity." Then he signed the other ball and said, "This one is for you." That's why Mike keeps all of those baseballs around. You can see them in the pillars there in his restaurant. He keeps them there for people to sign.

Lori said one time she played golf as a fill-in for Albert Pujols at a Charity Golf Tournament. Albert had become sick

---

*Red Sox principal owner, John Henry, a native of **QUINCY, ILLINOIS**, owned part of the Red Sox, Marlins and Yankees at the same time. Henry also spent part of his youth in Arkansas and wasn't able to play. She said their team actually used three of her golf balls for scoring purposes and she was shocked. She kept telling me how she saw "Bob." I said, "Bob who?" She said, "Bob Knight." I told her, "Bobby Knight!" I was born a Hoosier...of course, I know who Bobby Knight is... but I don't call him Bob. Calling Bobby Knight "Bob" is like calling Attila the Hun "Tilly"...

Mike Shannon was telling us that when he was in his younger playing days, the Cardinals had a private plane that was specifically for the Cardinals, like they do now. Half of the team went to the West Coast one day early and the other half flew out the next day. He said that he knew that his idol, Frank Sinatra, was going to be in Vegas. They talked the pilot into stopping in Las Vegas so they could see the concert. Mike was standing on the side of the stage watching and Frank actually said, "Hey everybody! We've got some people that we would like to introduce you to! This is Mike Shannon and the St. Louis Cardinals!" Mike said he just about died when **FRANK SINATRA*** knew his name. He said, "He didn't mention Stan Musial or any of the other guys who were big name players, he mentioned my name! That was the best day next to my wedding and the birth of my children!" His idol isn't even a baseball player, it's Frank Sinatra.

When I was a little girl, I fell in love with the Cardinals during the 1964 season. I watched or listened to every game. I remember sitting in my second grade classroom during the World Series fantasizing about my mother coming to get me out of school to go to the World Series. She never did. That has

---

*Bobby Thomson hit "The Shot Heard Around the World" on October 3, 1951...**FRANK SINATRA** and Jackie Gleason were at the game. When Thomson homered off Ralph Branca, Dodger fan Gleason did a technicolor yawn (vomited) on Sinatra's shoes...In the movie *The Godfather*, Sonny Corleone died while listening to that game... Dave Winfield was born that day.

always been my favorite team and that was my favorite season. When I was in college my brother and I went out to the clubs in the Soulard area. The beer distributor for my brother's fraternity came into the bar. He had just been to a bazillion-million barrel celebration at the brewery. I told him how much I loved the '64 Cardinals and that I remembered all the players and listened to every game. He told me that Mike Shannon would be soon coming into the bar and that he would introduce me. Sure enough, Mike Shannon came in and the beer distributor brought him over. He said, "You've got to meet this girl. She remembers all the '64 Cardinals." So Shannon asked me to name them. I started naming all the players until I got to right field. I said, "The right fielder is the only one I can't remember. I can't remember who played right field." Shannon said, "I did. Here's my ring to prove it." He took off his World Series ring, tossed it to me and walked away. Unfortunately, a few minutes later, someone must have told him, "Hey Shannon. You just gave away your World Series ring. Better go get it." He came back to get it. The next morning my brother told my Dad the story. My Dad thought that I had lied about not remembering who played right field just to be funny. I truly did not remember.

By the way, living in Cincinnati brings home how great Cardinal fans are. The Reds fans are the worst...fair-weather fans, only. When I go to St. Louis games in Cincinnati it's like a family reunion with all the Cardinal fans there.

—**Jody Shelden**, Cincinnati, Ohio

"HOME AGAIN"

Alex Mattman adds his autograph to the thousands of signatures already on the foul pole during the last game at Busch Stadium.

To the Best Fans In Baseball

*Thanks
for the memories*

BUSCH STADIUM

FINAL SEASON

1966 ★ 2005

™

Mike Matheny poses with a left-handed gold glove handed to him by a fan on Camera Day 2002. Notice the DK 57 on his cap in memory of his popular teammate Darryl Kile, who tragically passed away that season.

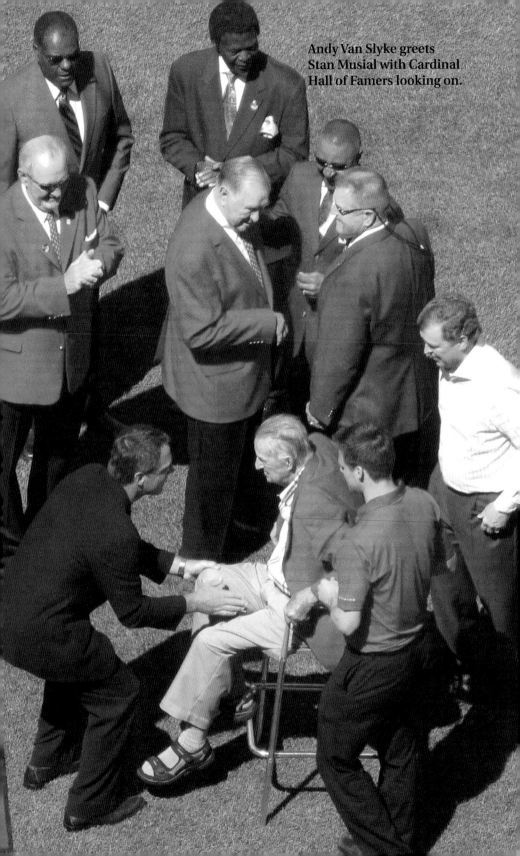

Andy Van Slyke greets
Stan Musial with Cardinal
Hall of Famers looking on.

Former Cardinals Andy Van Slyke and Boots Day share a bow with So Taguchi as Willie McGee and John Mabry look on.

Not even gloomy weather could reduce the glow of Opening Day at Busch Stadium in 2012

Bob Broeg congratulates Enos Slaughter on his statue dedication as fellow Hall of Famers Bob Gibson, Stan Musial, and Red Schoendienst look on.

Red Schoendienst (above) and Stan Musial (below) go for a ride.

Whitey Herzog enjoys his first day as a member of the Baseball Hall of Fame.

An unusual close-up shot of Yadi Molina in the bullpen

Hall of Famer Bob Gibson strikes a pose following his statue dedication ceremony.

The Clydesdales leave the old Busch Stadium for the last time

President John F. Kennedy greets Stan Musial at the 1962 All-Star Game in Washington, D.C.

Nine former Cardinals patrol outfield for the last time ever at the final game in the old Busch Stadium in 2005

The game's best players mingle with the fans at the 2009 All-Star Game in Busch Stadium

"FIFTY YEARS OF BROADCASTING"
1954 - 2004

SIGN HERE

B*rry B*nds' Autographs Are Selling Like Hotcakes... $2 A Stack

CARDINAL FEVER?
NO CURE!

DAVID MAYER

David Mayer, restaurant entrepreneur, is the ultimate Cardinal bobblehead collector with over 200. As a published columnist in Beckett's Hot Toys, *he wrote a column about Mark McGwire during his home run race in 1998. Mayer enjoys having his personal photographs autographed by the Cardinal players.*

I try to get down to Springfield, MO, several times a year for some Cardinal minor league games. I have gone to Quad Cities a couple times also to watch the River Bandits. That is a beautiful park. It's a picture-perfect park the way it looks out onto the Mississippi. It is really nice. The Quad Cities is a great area.

I'm an autograph collector too. I like to take pictures and get them signed because it's something personal—something no one else is going to have. One night in the Quad Cities, I saw Shelby Miller, our first-round pick in 2009, sitting in the twentieth row behind home plate with the radar gun. My buddy and I walked over and sat in the open seats near him. In between innings we were talking to him. He said, "Yeah, I'm doing this. This is part of my job today." He was just in plain clothes clocking pitches from the opposing team. I asked him if he would sign a couple of autographs for us and he said, "Oh, sure! Sure!" In between innings, he signed things for me and for the guy who was with me. He was a very, very nice person, and very open. He explained what he was doing and gave us a little education on what his job was when he was not pitching. It was a pretty neat experience...

I've been fortunate enough to have been to several All-Star Games, but I like the Home Run Derbies more. The FanFest is great as well. It's a great way to interact with different people in the community and it gives you a different perspective on baseball. Things have changed over the past ten years. The car companies used to be friendlier and would give away all kinds of promo items and gifts. They had good prizes, however, they've gotten a lot cheaper over the last couple of years. One thing I did at the 2009 All-Star festivities, which I have never done but have always wanted to, was to volunteer. If you have a few days of vacation time or time to get away from work to volunteer, it's a blast!

I signed up to volunteer and the Cardinals picked me! They took us all down to Busch Stadium to go through an orientation. Once orientation was completed, they called you back to let you know if you were accepted. If you were accepted, next you had to complete a training class. They gave you a shirt, a fanny pack, and a badge that would let you come and go, so the days that you weren't working at FanFest you could come and see everything for free. That was great!

I was picked to work the autograph booth, which, of course, I thought was great! To volunteer, you had to work three days, at least five hours a day. Basically, all we did was direct the people through the lines. In the past, it was a nightmare. They used to have one line and one table with three or four people signing. After an hour those people moved out and four more people moved in to sign. If you were in a line for over an hour, you didn't necessarily get autographs from who was originally at the table. In 2009, they changed it. There were four different autograph tables so if you wanted to get an autograph from Jack Clark, for example, you would go get in that line. We knew approximately how many people we could get through the line in two hours. After we got to that amount of people we would cut the line off, so if you were already standing in line, you were guaranteed an autograph. After all of the fans got their autographs, we were able to get our stuff signed and we got to meet the players. Jack Clark, aka "The Ripper", was a very nice guy and he thanked us for helping out. I also met Lee Smith when I got to work his booth. He wasn't personalizing items but would let you take a photo and also was giving out photos of himself he had previously signed.

While working, this guy comes walking up to the booth. I knew who he was but the two other guys working with me didn't. They said, "Sorry, sir. You've got to get in line. You can't get in there!" I asked them, "Don't you know who that is? That's Rollie Fingers!" They were apologetic, "Oh! Mr. Fingers!" Well, he had three pictures that he had with Lee Smith and he wanted Lee to sign them. Lee was floored, he said, "YOU want ME to sign those pictures? Really?" Then I asked Rollie if I could get a picture with him and he said, "Sure." So we're having our picture taken and Lee's peeking around the corner looking at us. It was really funny! Lee was just stunned that Rollie had come up to ask him for his autograph when it should have been the other way around. It was a real good time!

Wainwright is one of the nicest guys on the team as far as signing autographs. He's also hilarious when he's around his teammates, playing jokes on them. Adam likes to stop and sign autographs for people—he is really good about that. One day he came in and I said, "Hey Adam! Trivia question!" He said, "What?" I said, "Which one of your teammates has a birthday today?" He was thinking about it and said, "I don't know?" I said, "That's alright. I'm going to give you some brownie points to get you in good with him. Today's Chris Carpenter's birthday." He was happy to learn that tidbit.

When Brendan Ryan was here, he was a really good guy. He would sign autographs all of the time too. Early on, when he first got called up, he was driving this old beater of a car. The fans who were waiting for autographs were saying, "That's not a player...that's not a player!" Then all of a sudden he stops and rolls down the window of this little car and signs for people.

It looked like a car that you would just buy off of a car lot for $800...it was a pretty cheap car! Obviously, eventually, he bought a new vehicle.

I like unique collectibles...something somebody else may not have. I have a limited edition, renowned artist, Rick Rush print. It's numbered and signed by Rick Rush and it's called, "*Out of Character.*" He did it after the Cardinals won the World Series in '06. It starts with Reyes, it's like he's starting to get ready for the wind up. It goes from Anthony Reyes, then it has Carpenter, Suppan, Weaver and then Wainwright. It's full body drawings of each player in the motion of actually throwing a pitch. At the end of it, you have Molina. In the background you can see Albert throwing the ball and off to the left it has Eckstein. So you have all of the key players from that Series. They made two thousand and six of them. I took mine to the Stadium to get it signed.

The first person to sign it was Adam Wainwright. He gave me a nice autograph. When Milwaukee was in town, I caught up with Suppan and he gave me a real nice signature on it also. When Jeff Weaver came in town, I got down there late. I had my print with me. As I was walking up, I asked, "Hey, has anybody seen Weaver?" A guy said, "Yeah, he just got done signing autographs and he's across the street on a golf cart." I went running up the sidewalk and sure enough, he was sitting in the golf cart. He's was getting ready to take off and I yelled, "Jeff.... Jeff...hold on! One more! One more!" He said, "I've gotta go!" But he looked up and saw me with this big 16x20 print. Thankfully, he said, "Hold on a second. Hold on, I gotta sign this for this guy." He was just looking at the print, taking it all in. It's a really, really neat print. He ended up signing it across the top, right between where Suppan and Wainwright signed. He was really nice. "Man, this is a pretty nice picture!" If it was a card or ball, I don't think he would have stopped.

I also go to **SPRING TRAINING***. In Jupiter, along the Cardinals side where the players come into the park, there is a driveway. Sometimes when the players leave after the game, they will stop and roll down the window and sign autographs. A lot of fans and autograph people hang out there to try to get their favorite Cardinals' autographs. I was just hanging out after the game, taking it easy, seeing what's going on. A guy comes walking out about an hour after the game was over with a skateboard under his arm. I knew right off the bat who it was, but nobody else seemed to know. I said, "Hey Brian! What's going on?" It

*In a 1925 **SPRING TRAINING** game, Babe Ruth played for the Philadelphia A's along with Jimmy Foxx, Lefty Grove, Al Simmons and Mickey Cochrane. Ruth went 0 for 3, and it's undetermined why he happened to play for the A's that day instead of the home team, Yankees.

was Brian Anderson! He said, "Not much! It was a pretty good game." He was very nice and signed some things for me. I was talking to him while he signed and then he asked, "Does anyone else want an autograph?" Some of the people didn't even know who he was! When he was done signing he said, "Alright! I'll see you guys later!" Then he flops his skateboard down, hops onto it and skates down the street along the side of the Stadium in Jupiter. I've never seen a baseball player do that!

It was maybe a year later when I saw him down at Busch. "Hey Brian, do you still do skateboarding?" He looked like he was thinking, "How do you know?" He smiled and laughed and said, "Yeah, a little bit still."

Ozzie's Restaurant was in Westport Plaza in Maryland Heights for years. When you walked in, there was all kinds of sports memorabilia—artifacts hanging on the walls signed by the different players. The neatest thing was this big display case that held all of Ozzie's Gold Gloves. Some items belonged to the restaurant, however, some of the things were Ozzie's personal items he was loaning to the restaurant. His son, Nikko, was up there with two of his friends the night the placed closed for good. They were going to take the gloves back to Ozzie's house. Nikko and each of his friends had a Gold Glove and took them out to their van. When they came back in for a few more. I asked him, "Hey Nikko, is there any way that I could hold one of those? It would be pretty cool!" Nikko said, "Sure! Come on over here!" I was able to get a picture of me holding the glove with two hands on one side of the glove and Nikko has his hand on the other side of it. That was a unique opportunity that you don't get very often. Later that evening, Ozzie was thanking everybody for coming out. He posed for tons of pictures and signed lots of autographs. He was extremely nice. But later on in the evening, it finally hit him that this was it. He got emotional. It was such a fun place to hang out!

Speaking of restaurants, about four years ago, Jimmy Edmonds and a friend of his, Mark Winfield, opened a restaurant here in St. Louis called *"Club 15."* One night, around the All-Star Game in July 2009, my friends and I were there eating dinner. We heard that Jimmy was in town and that he might be at his restaurant later that evening so we brought some stuff for him to sign. While we were eating, he was walking around asking everyone, "How's the food? How's everything?" He saw that we had brought some stuff and was just incredible! He actually sat down at the table and talked with us for about ten minutes. His wife was there with their two little kids who were running around. My friend knew that his family might be there too, so my friend brought one of his Jimmy Edmonds bobblehead dolls that they gave out at the Stadium. He brought it for Jimmy to give to his kids. He had it sealed up in a Tupperware container, wrapped up so it would not get broken. He told him, "Jimmy, I want you to have this for your son. I'm sure that he'll enjoy it somewhere down the road." Jimmy said, "Aww, hey, I really appreciate it!" Jimmy takes the bobblehead out, puts it on the table and it starts bobbing. His little kid said, "Look! There's Daddy! There's Daddy! Look!" We were all just cracking up! It was a great evening! I had about six things and he signed everything we had....just beautiful autographs. I also had a World Series ball and every player that I get to sign it, I ask them to write "'06" after their name. He was like, "Why would you want that on there? It says 2006 right on the ball! Can't you read?" He was just joking with me. He was awesome...just a super nice guy! The food was great at his restaurant. It's a good place to go if you're looking to eat somewhere in St. Louis, and if Edmonds is in town, you're sure to get his autograph.

AS A YOUNGSTER HE PRAYED TO BE A CARDINAL. GOD ANSWERED HIS PRAYERS: HE SAID, "NO." LITTLE TIMMY DOLAN PRAYED TO BE A CARDINAL. GOD SAID, "YES!"

TERRY RUSH

Terry Rush is the pastor at the Church of Christ in Tulsa, Oklahoma. He is also the author of two excellent books. The first is Silver Voice, Golden Heart—*a nifty book on Jack Buck. His latest book* MVP *is an inspirational home run for youngsters. St. Louis native (Ballwin), Tim Dolan, was named a U.S. Catholic Cardinal for the New York Archdiocese in 2012.*

Every year, I attend the Cardinals Legends Camp in Jupiter, Florida, for a week. Two years ago, Ozzie Smith was going to be there for the very first time. I was curious as to whether or not we'd connect because with me being a minister, sometimes the players stay their distance—and I don't blame them. As I unpacked my gear in the hotel in Jupiter that first day, I realized that my glove is an Ozzie Smith model—a six finger Rawlings.

Ozzie walked by and I said, "Ozzie, come here a minute. I've got a problem here." He said, "What's that?" I said, "I've got an Ozzie Smith model glove and it doesn't catch the ball!" He repeated, "It doesn't catch the ball?" I said, "No. Something must be wrong with the glove, and it's a beautiful glove." He said, "Well, hey, let me use it during the game and let's just see." He used my glove during the ballgame—it made my whole week and it was only the first day. He made it just dance! It was amazing! At the end of the game, he brought it back to me and said, "Hey, Terry, it's not the arrow, it's the Indian!" I said, "Really?" He said, "Yeah!" He laughed and we went on.

I wanted to get that get that glove signed by Ozzie before the week was over. We reached the Saturday night banquet. We were going to play two games on Sunday and then go home. On Saturday night, they made an announcement at the end of dinner: "No more autographs from Ozzie or Lou Brock. You guys have worn them out. Please do not ask any more." I'm sitting there thinking..."What am I going to do? I really want that Ozzie Smith glove autographed by him."

When the banquet was over, I walked up to him. He was visiting with some former players and campers. I called him over and said, "Hey Ozzie. I want to tell you something. I won't sign your glove tomorrow." He just went right along with me and said, "What? Terry, I want you to sign my glove!" I said, "Not tomorrow, Ozzie. I'm not signing." I walked off and went to my room.

The next morning at 6:30, we were in the lobby waiting for the bus to transport us to the stadium in Jupiter when Ozzie called to me from clear across the lobby and said, "Hey, Terry! Please sign my glove today?" All the guys are starting to notice the banter, and I said, "No Ozzie. I told you last night that I'm not signing on Sunday!" he said, "Oh, Terry, please?" I said, "I'm not signing, Ozzie." We went to the stadium and after breakfast, we ran into each other and he said, "Terry, really, would you sign my glove today?" I said, "Ozzie, I'm not signing." Then I paused and said, "I might sign it in front of everyone in the camp, but probably not."

An hour later, we had our camp meeting and our team meetings. Ozzie got up with his glove and a Sharpie pen and said,

"The only think I want from camp is for Terry Rush to sign my glove and he won't sign it." He said, "Terry, would you sign it for me." I said, "No." He said, "Oh, please, Terry?" I said, "No. I can't Ozzie." Then he responds, "But I really wanted you to." I got up acting like I'm just dying because I have to do this thing and signed the glove in front of everyone. They all applauded, and it was really neat and such an honor for me to do that. When the games were over, we were all packed and heading to the airport when I ran into Ozzie one more time in the corridor and said, "Hey Ozzie! I know I can't ask, but will you sign my glove for me?" He said, "Hey Terry, you signed my glove for me, I'll sign for you." I ended up getting his autograph on my glove, and it is now a monument in my office.

A photographer at the camp snapped an extremely good picture of Ozzie up in the air above a guy sliding into second. He's making the double play throw to first base. The ball was about ten feet out from Ozzie's outstretched arm. One of the players said, "Terry, look at the picture." I said, "Yeah, isn't that great?" He said, "No. Look at the picture!" I looked, and right in the center is Ozzie's glove with my autograph on it! Ozzie said he had never asked for an autograph before...just mine...

My latest book is entitled "MVP-Why You're the Most Valuable in God's Eyes". The book has two scenarios in it where it ties faith with baseball. Many of the Cardinal old-timers endorsed the book: Tommy Herr, the late Bob Forsch, Whitey Herzog and others which means a lot to me. Some of the other players let me tell stories about them—Bob Tewksbury, for instance, and Ricky Horton who's now a broadcaster with the Cardinals. The idea of "MVP-Why You're the Most Valuable in God's Eyes" is to encourage the underdog. Everyone struggles at some point in their life, feeling like they're not good enough. MVP is a book that just keeps repeating and drilling into our thought process that we are most important—very valuable. It has a lot of biblical illustrations of people who are underdogs, and God will help bring them through. Every person, regardless of how successful or how prominent they become, wonders at times, "Is there something really good about me?" This book addresses this and it's a home run. It draws people into the fact that the spiritual side of life really does count. It's really important. When a person gets discouraged, it's not because they have a leg cramp or sore elbow, they're getting discouraged in their heart. That's the proof of the spiritual side of life. *MVP* says, "Regardless of what you think about yourself, you're more important than that. God is not out to get you, He's out to help you and He'll do it."

Next year will be my 30th fantasy camp. I haven't missed any. I was the rookie of rookies and was going to go only one time. I never dreamed that I would get to go again. It has, of course, been thrilling for me to get to know these Cardinal players personally; to realize that they're ordinary men with ordinary struggles. They have good hearts. Al Hrabosky is one of my dearest friends in these camps. He has a heart that runs wide open to help people. That's what I see all the time. There are, on occasion, one or two players that are a little bit of a pain, but most of them are so real. It's so much fun to see that. The talent surprised me. I was in camp for about an hour and had thought, "I might have been able to play ball if I'd only had the right breaks"...no way! The human heart side of these guys is what I've really enjoyed—from **BOB GIBSON*** to Rex Hudler—they're good to me. They're good to us and very patient with us. They've become good friends.

The challenge when I began going to these fantasy camps was, "Will I be able to throw from third to first?" Now, the challenge is, "Will I be able to see from third to first?"

***BOB GIBSON** considered Cub Billy Williams his toughest "out" and Sandy Koufax stated that former Cardinal, Gene Oliver, was his toughest "out."

QUICK HITS AND INTERESTING BITS

Any time you and your buddies got your name in the *Suburban Journal*, it was always neat. To see your picture in there was a really big deal. You'd think, "How great would it be if I could make the *Post-Dispatch* sports page or *The Sporting News*?" Back when I was in high school, my family went down to Spring Training and my mom brought me home a program signed by a few of the Cardinal players and announcers. She had a nice little conversation with Al Hrabosky because he was walking past after Jack Buck had signed her program. She knew that he was someone with the Cardinals but didn't know who. She said, "You can sign it if you want to." He said, "If I want to?" She said, "Yeah. I just don't recognize you!" She was chuckling and he walked over and signed it, "Al Hrabosky, the Mad Hungarian". She brought this program home to me and it was a big deal to me!

Every year the *Post-Dispatch* would do a special annual baseball section. You could get all the information about every team's schedule and a break-down of each team, who their players were and their forecast. On the inside of the special baseball section was Mom's picture, leaning over the rail; laughing with Al Hrabosky and getting the autograph on the program she brought me. I said, "That's amazing! I play all these sports, and my Mom makes the sports page before I do! Not only is it the sports page, but a special section of the sports page!"

A few years later, the St. Louis Blues traded for Wayne Gretzky and my sister was on the front page of the sports page with her friend. There was a great photo of Wayne Gretzky leaning against the glass before his first game as a Blue. He was looking up at the scoreboard as my sister and her friend were tapping on the glass trying to get his attention! That picture made the paper.

Within a short period of time, there were my sister and my mom on the sports pages and I never could get in the paper.

My first time in the paper, was in *The Journal* and I was eating a chicken wing at Bass Pro Shops in St. Charles! What an athlete I was!

—**Danny Pence**, St. Charles, MO

Enos Slaughter was Mr. Hustle and I always got a kick out of watching him play when I was a little boy. I was at a game when I was about ten and was interested in getting autographs. There were a bunch of kids there. I was a rookie at all of this and didn't really know what to do. A lot of the kids were edging in to get in front of the line. I really didn't know how to do that yet, so I just stood back and watched. Enos was signing autographs and was talking to the kids, and then all of a sudden he said, "I'm sorry, I have to leave now." He had signed a lot of scorecards, and I was still standing there just watching. I thought, "Well, I guess I have to do a little more next time to get closer!"

Enos started to leave and I followed him hoping I could get up enough nerve to ask him to sign my scorecard. He was leaving the gate, and I was a little bit behind him. He started walking up the street because he was staying at the Fairgrounds Hotel. I was about 15 feet behind him. I had to pick up the pace to keep up with him. He stopped and turned around and I stopped, too. He motioned for me to come so of course I did! He asked, "Do you want something from me, son?" I had the scorecared in my hand. He said, "I bet I know what you want!" I said, "Yes sir, would you sign my scorecard, please?" He said, "Why don't you just come along with me?" We walked another block while talking about the Cardinals. He said, "Tell you what! Why don't you come on in and we'll sit down in the lobby and we'll talk a little bit more about the Cardinal game today." I sat in a big chair at the Fairgrounds Hotel in the lobby right there by Forest Park and Natural Bridge with Enos Slaughter. He was very cordial, very nice and he seemed like he had plenty of time to talk to me. He asked me if I was going to be a good Cardinal fan. I said, "Yes sir, I am!" We sat there and talked for over and hour.

Years later, I was at the statue unveiling ceremony of Enos Slaughter at Busch Stadium. He was a man that I thought a lot of as a player, and I wanted to see his statue. I got down there very early to position myself to get a good photo of him at the statue. As things developed, all of the Hall of Famers started to appear: Bob Gibson, Stan Musial, Red Schoendienst and Bob Broeg, as well as Enos. I was all set for the picture, and just at the moment I wanted to take a shot, a person next to me raised their hand to wave leaving me with the greatest picture of someone's hand. The man standing next to me got a perfect shot because I didn't bother him! He knew I was upset because I had been standing in that position for a good hour and a half to get that shot! Another man next to me saw what happened and said to me „If you would like a copy of that picture, I would be glad to send you one!" I gave him my address and told him that I would sure appreciate it if he would. He did send it to me and I'm so glad to have that picture. I still have it on my desk.

—**Don Dempski**, St. Peters, MO

Back in 1986, my buddy Lee and I went down to the Stadium to watch the Mets/Cardinals game. I was 15 and he was 16. We took his old white Cutlass down to the Stadium that we called it "The Ghost" with its big C.B. antenna on the trunk. Back then, we never had tickets to games—Lee could get us into anything. That was one of the games where someone with a stamped hand, licked it, and then pressed it onto our hands so we didn't have to pay to get in. Anyway, we 'weaseled' good seats and watched the game.

Lee was a huge autograph guy, and I could never get him to leave the Stadium. After the game, we were waiting around and he saw Dwight Gooden coming out with a huge crowd of fans. As we crossed the street to the Marriott, I was watching all the people in the crowd and not looking at the traffic. Thankfully, Gooden was watching and reached out and pulled me back out of the way of car coming down the street. Since then I've always told people that Dwight Gooden saved my life! Lee had a *Sports Illustrated* for him to sign but his pen ran out of ink. Gooden apologized and moved on to the next autograph.

Lee was so disappointed and wanted to hang around longer. Like I said earlier, I could never get him to leave because he always thought there was a chance for more autographs. Personally, the only one I ever wanted to get was **TITO*** Landrum's. An hour or so later, Lee went into the Marriott to use the restroom and came out with a gigantic smile. While in there, he peed while standing between Darryl Strawberry and Dwight Gooden. He showed me his **SPORTS ILLUSTRATED*** signed by both of them. I joked that I hoped he let them wash their hands first! When he showed it to his uncle, his uncle's only words were, 'I bet you had the smallest willy of the three!"

—**Marc Anderson**, Woodstock, CT; St. Louis native

I've never been one for autographs, in fact, I don't really take many pictures—I just store things in my head a whole lot. I did keep the newspapers from when they won the Series. I cut out the McClellan headline "Kyle is Perfect" and gave that to my friend whose name is Kyle. I put it on his door, actually, and he kept it there for a while. Then he moved it into his office and he kept it! Now I'm thinking, "Man! I'd like to have that back now!" I didn't even have

***TITO** Fuentes of the Giants once warned opposing pitchers not to throw at him because "I'm the father of five or six kids."

***SPORTS ILLUSTRATED** rated New York City circa 1966 as the worst time and place to be a sports fan. The Yankees, Knicks and Rangers finished last, the Mets escaped last place for the first time and the Giants were 1–12–1. The best time and place to be a sports fan according to Sports Illustrated: Philadelphia, 1980.

tickets to save from this World Series because we got it online. It was the first World Series I had gone to. The one ticket I do have from Busch Stadium is when the **BEATLES**[*] were there.

—**Sue Tretter**, Lindenwood University

Weinhardt's Party Rentals did a lot of big party set-ups for both corporate and residential parties. On one occasion, Jack Buck's wife called and hired us for a big party she was having. When we delivered all of the product, Mrs. Buck was there. Joe Buck was in college at the time, and he came strolling down the steps... just like a regular 'ole college kid. It was interesting to see them in their normal environment.

When it came time to pick everything up after the party on that Monday, I made sure I was the one who grabbed it. I was really excited—I was a huge Jack Buck fan! I went to their house really early in the morning; probably a little too early. There was a side door by the garage, right off the driveway, which connected to the kitchen. I knocked on the door, and to my surprise, who opened it but Jack Buck. When he opened the door, he was just in a robe and slippers and his hair was a little disheveled. I said, "Oh, Mr. Buck! Am I too early? I apologize!" He said, "No...no...no. Come on in! I was just having a cup of coffee right now—do you want a cup? Here...sit down with me. I'll even give you the sports page!" I started laughing and said, "I can't do that, but that would be really awesome, and I appreciate the offer!"

[*]The **BEATLES**' last concert ever was at Candlestick Park in San Francisco on August 29, 1966. It lasted 33 minutes.

I started picking up all of the equipment and loaded it up in the truck. When I got finished, he was sitting reading his paper and drinking his cup of coffee. As I got ready to leave, I went in to tell him that I was done. I had to ask him, "Hey, I hate to bother you and I usually don't do this, but I'm just a really huge fan of yours. Is there any possible way that I could grab an autograph from you?" He said, "Oh sure! Let me go get a press photo." I said, "Well...if it's no problem? I really don't want to bother you?" He left the room and when he walked back in he said, "Listen, I don't have any more press photos, but I have this." He then handed me an autographed baseball of everybody on the entire team when **JOE TORRE*** was managing the team! It had Ozzie Smith's autograph, Lee Smith, Tewksbury, and right under Joe Torre's name Jack Buck signed! I was so excited! I couldn't believe it and I just thanked him profusely.

I took off back to work in our work truck. I was driving as fast as I could so I could show everybody back at work my ball when I was pulled over by the Des Peres police. When the cop pulled me over, he said, "Do you know how fast you were going?" I said to him, "Look what I got! Jack Buck gave me his autograph!" He just looked at me and just signed the ticket, "Slow down." I went on to work and told everybody, and of course, I had to pay the ticket! I had never met Jack Buck before but his voice sounded exactly like he does on the radio. It was cool! It was one of my biggest memories!

—**Lou Viviano**, No longer employed at Weinhardt's Party Rentals in Des Peres, MO

After the annual Baseball Writers Dinner ended, everybody would gather around the table and get autographs from the celebrities. Many times Musial would stick around the longest

---

***JOE TORRE** was player/manager of the Mets for eighteen days in 1977. Since 1962 there have been four player/managers with Pete Rose (1984-86) the last...In 1935 there were nine player/managers.

while the other guys would jet out of there. You could walk around and say hello to each player and get their autograph. Well, Musial is staying around signing autographs and he has a little contingent around him at the two main tables. People were coming up to the stage and they were putting their picture or whatever they had to get autographed up on the table.

Every once in a while someone would snap a photo of Stan. He would take the program, roll it up like a bat and get into his classic pose, like he was batting again. He would pose and people would snap photos.

He mentioned that he could sign his name with both hands. I had given him an 8x10 photo that I had gotten from my grandfather who worked at the Stadium when Stan retired. They gave out these 8x10s with all Stan's stats and baseball clippings. Musial said, "What's your name?" He signed the picture, "To Craig, Best Wishes. Stan Musial". He said, "Do you mind if I turn this over and sign the back with my right hand?" I said, "Wait. I'll get another." I reached into my bag and handed him another photo and he signed it right-handed. He held it up and said, "Ha! Ha! Ha! Ha! You didn't think I could do it! Did you?" I got two 8x10 autographs from Musial and if you compared them, you wouldn't know the difference. When you look at it close, you can see some of the details differ very slightly but you really can't tell just by looking.

—**Don Sullivan**, Atlanta, GA

In '87, when the Cardinals played the Twins, their star player was Kirby Puckett. He was a short, round guy. Normally there were just two buses for visiting teams, but because of the World Series going on, there were a lot of other vehicles. We were trying to figure out where the players are going to be coming out and which bus they're going to get on. We noticed Puckett getting his shoes shined. There were a lot of people gathered around him, but you can't really see him that well because he's not that tall. He was standing there right on the sidewalk in a suit, and he has his foot up on a wooden box. At Busch Stadium, there used to be these shoe shine boys—you would see

202 FOR CARDINAL FANS ONLY!

this a lot in the '80's. They would carry around these wooden boxes and shine the players' shoes. They would frequently be given tickets to the game. Some of these kids would use the tickets to go in. Some of the kids would use the tickets to sell to make a little money. A lot of these kids that would go to the game had a pretty good rapport with the players, so they would get bats and batting gloves and things like that.

A couple of the shoe shine boys are shining up Kirby's shoes, and talking to him. A lot of people are gathered around, so we walked over there to get a look at Kirby Puckett. As good as he was, he wasn't that tall of a guy, but he was really round. He looked like a shorter version of Charles Barkley. We're standing there hoping to shake Kirby's hand and get his autograph. He's talking to people just like he's one of the people out there. He's not big-timing anybody and he's not trying to keep people away from him.

There were these little girls, who were about fourteen years old. They were looking at Kirby and saying, "Aw, look at Kirby...isn't he cute? Look at Kirby." They were talking about him like he was a puppy. He would just keep talking to them and they kept saying, "Aw, look at how cute he is!" He was talking to these girls just like they were people he went to school with or something. I assume the Cardinals were up at the time because they kept asking him, "Kirby are you sad? Are you sad, Kirby?" Kirby told them, "No, I'm a professional ball player. I play in the Major Leagues for the Minnesota Twins, and I play center-field and I'm never going to be sad."
After Kirby was done with getting his shoes shined, we got Kirby's autograph, then he got on the bus and away they went.

—**Paul Andrews**, Little Rock

Back in the mid '80s, baseball collector shows were real popular. There were lots of memorabilia and baseball card stores. A collector show at the Holiday Inn by the airport would fill up a big meeting room plus the Holidome out by the pool with tables and tables of memorabilia, pictures, cards...anything you could think involving baseball you could go buy or trade. Back then, the autographs weren't as crazy as they are now. You would pay $2.50 for an admission ticket, and with that you could get an autograph of whoever was attending that particular event. Well, in the mid '80s, they would roll people in there like Lou Brock, Curt Flood, Dal Maxvill, Joe Torre, Bob Gibson and even a couple of out of town guys like Bob Feller, Warren Spahn, Hank Aaron, Willie Mays. For $2.50, you could walk on stage with your admission ticket and get an autograph from each of those guys at the table. There were never less than five people at those tables and a lot of them were Hall of Famers or Rookies of the Year. This was 1985-1987. I'll never forget, as a teenager, getting to walk across the stage and shake hands with Curt Flood, Hank Aaron and Willie Mays. When I shook hands with Willie Mays, it felt like his fingertips were up on my forearm. He had really big hands.

In the late '80s, they started raising admission prices and had separate autograph prices, where you had to buy an autograph ticket. Early on it was $5-$10 for an autograph ticket....
—**Dick Morris**, Springfield, MO

Johnny Londoff was a Chevrolet dealer in St. Louis. Back in the '80s, a lot of the Cardinal players would have a commercial affiliation with Johnny Londoff. You would see Ozzie Smith on Johnny Londoff Chevrolet commercials and hear Ozzie on the radio, also. Every once in a while, the players would be at autograph sessions around the cars in the showroom. Fans would be lined up out the door and down the sidewalk, and into the street if they had to. One time, it was Ozzie, Willie McGee and George Hendrick. I was a huge George Hendrick fan—loved his batting style and his goofy pants being too long. They always referred to George as Silent George. I never heard him talk! I had no idea what his voice sounded like...no idea! We're at Johnny Londoff Chevrolet, and we had been standing in line a while. As we got up along the building, we could see Ozzie, Willie and George sitting inside. Back then, there weren't as many player appearances. There weren't as many charity events and there weren't as many interactions with players and kids, so to see those guys up close was a big deal! They were the guys you looked up to as Cardinal players. We stood outside the glass, waiting our turn. Every once in a while they'd turn around and look outside. If they made eye contact, it was cool because that was your player...that was your team. Every once in a while, Ozzie would lean over to say something to Hendrick and Hendrick would lean back in his chair and look out the window like he was trying to see how long the line was. He would do this about every 10 minutes as the line was creeping up to the door and we were getting ready to make our way inside. We didn't know if we were going to make it to the front of the line.

We get in the doors and we're getting up close to the table. You could bring something for them to sign or they had promo pictures there that they would sign. It was neat because they would spend a little bit more time talking to you—they were sitting down and comfortable. We're getting up close to the table and we know a lot of people aren't going to make it through the line to get autographs—they're going to have to cut the line off somewhere. We're up close to the table, when George leans back in his chair. Again, I had never heard him talk. Ozzie leans over and says something to him, and he leans back and I heard George talk for the first time in my life. "This ship sails in five minutes!" That told me we were getting his autograph, but everybody outside in the line was going to be disappointed because they had been there two hours. My buddy and I were so excited that we made the cut—we were going to get to get up close to Willie, Ozzie and George.

There wasn't much conversation, but they signed a nice autograph for us. It was a big deal because it was all three guys and a good signature. Anybody that tries to get an autograph at the ballpark knows those players are in a hurry. Before the game, you might get a nice signature, but after the game, the players are in a hurry. You might get a half of signature or an initial. To get a nice signature, usually with a personalization meant a lot. They at least took the time to hear your name.

A lot of people around town probably have those black and white photos that say "Johnny Londoff Chevrolet" and have autographs on them.

—**Jimmy Hensley**, Alton, IL

In 1985, the Cardinals had beaten the Mets in a big series in September. It was late in the season. It was always neat to stand outside the glass doors where the players would come out. The buses would park right on the sidewalk and the players would have to come out through the crowd. If it wasn't a big game, you could interact with them. But with the pennant chase going on, they had barricades up. There were a lot more people out there. Not only were they along the barricades, they were also up top on the main walkway. This was at the old Busch Stadium. As players would come out, everybody would chant their name or yell something to them. The big thing back then was whenever a team would get eliminated from the playoffs, everyone would sing, "Na na na na na, Na na na na na, Hey, hey, hey, goodbye!" It would get louder and louder. My buddy and I used to love that song—it was one of our favorite songs. In the mid '80s, we got to sing it to a lot of teams that were no longer in the playoff run. The whole crowd was out there chanting and singing this song. It was neat to see the star players. Gooden comes out...Howard Johnson...Keith Hernandez. You could barely see in the tinted windows of the bus who was sitting where and who was sitting by whom. Strawberry was sitting in the seat close to the aisle, away from the glass. As everyone is chanting, there are kids on dads' shoulders and people holding up signs. Right as the bus pulls off, you could see Strawberry lean over and flip the bird at someone who was taunting him.

That was the year that the "David Letterman Show" had the phrase that became famous, "The Mets are Pond Scum" There were t-shirts and buttons and anything you wanted. It was crazy! You see those guys—usually in a positive light— and you never see them react. You never see anyone get mad.

Here's this young guy—Darryl Strawberry—who is a super, young, talented player that had a great future ahead of him, and he's really upset that the fans are getting on him. He showed a lot of emotion and leaned over and gave the bird. Strawberry now actually lives in the St. Louis area. He became part of a St. Peters church and is active in that community. It's nice to see he turned it around.

—**Joe Liddy**, Dublin, OH

CARDINAL PALOOZA

Open the Gates and Open Them Wide, Redbird Fans are Coming Inside

A COACH IS A TEACHER...
WITH A DEATH WISH

BOB BENBEN

Bob Benben was born and raised in Chicago and moved to St. Louis in 1957. He graduated from Mercy High School and played freshman baseball and basketball at Mizzou. Benben graduated from Washington University. He has coached high school baseball in the St. Louis area and also was a scout for the St. Louis Cardinals.

The summer before we moved to St. Louis, I worked at Hoyne Playground which is part of the Chicago Parks and Recreation System. Rogers Hornsby worked for the recs system and he came to Hoyne Playground. I coached Little League Baseball there and I helped run a clinic with Rogers Hornsby. He looked like he was 100 years old, he was tan and his face was leathery. He was an old codger to me. One time I asked him, "How do you get out of a slump?" He said, "Well, I bunt. I watch the ball hit the bat and I separate my hands like Ty." I said, "Ty?" He said, "Yeah, Ty Cobb." That was my first brush with a Cardinal Hall of Famer.

My first taste of coaching success was when I was coaching Augustinian Academy, the Fighting Braves. We were playing Ritenour in 1967 for the State Championship down at **HEINE MEINE PARK***. We were taking batting practice in the cage down the right field line when all of a sudden, this guy yells, "Hey

*Heine Meine Field is located at Little Broadway and Lemay Ferry Road. The park contains almost ten acres and is named for Heine Meine, a Major League pitcher 70 years ago who owned the bar that was adjacent to the field for many years.

Bobby, Bobby, Bobby!" I turned around and it was Cardinal Hall of Famer Joe Medwick! When I played at Wash U, Medwick was the Assistant Coach for Roy Lee at St. Louis University so he knew who I was. I said, "Hey! How are you doing?" He responded, "I heard you have a pretty good player?" I said, "Yeah, a catcher named Jim Wosman! He's in there hitting right now." Wosman ended up being a third round draft choice with the Tigers that year. Medwick is standing there watching him in the cages. Someone comes over to see me for a minute and when I turned back around, there Medwick was in the cage working with Wosman. He's telling him where to place his hands on the bat and doing all this coaching, so I yell, "Joe! Get out of there! Hey, we're playing in thirty minutes and you're trying to coach the kid…you're going to screw him up!" That was my second brush with a Cardinal Hall of Famer.

I scouted for the Cardinals for a number of years. I was what was known as a commission scout. I scouted a pitcher named Danny Hitt. He was my first signing. I had recommended him to the Cardinals and they drafted him as a late draft pick. I've had 15 kids that have signed but only a couple that made it to the Big Leagues. Of all the other kids that have signed—Vogel, Manna, Richardson, Lenny Klaus—they all did fine but they weren't going to make it to the Big Leagues. Wosman, Bryan Oelkers and Scott Cooper were the ones that made it

I had a supervisor named Tom McCormick. One day he calls me up and said, "Bob what are you doing this afternoon? Meet me over at Country Day. I want you to take a look at a player over there with me." So I met him over there and it was Joe Buck pitching. Tom introduced me to Jack Buck and his wife Carol. We sat and watched Joe Buck pitch and then gave them an evaluation about what we thought about Joe as a prospect. He wasn't bad—he was good. We recommended that he needed to go on to college to get more experience. He did go to

INDIANA*, but I didn't really follow him because it was out of my area. I don't know if he pitched much at Indiana, if at all. We just thought that he needed more seasoning.

When you met Jack Buck, it was like he already knew you. He was a classy person, just an unbelievable guy! I would really like to sit down and talk to Joe sometime and tell him about my experience with his Dad but I've never had that opportunity.

I coached high school for several years. As far as statistics are concerned, I tell my players, "Boys, statistics are important but I look at statistics like a bikini on a woman..it shows a lot but it doesn't show everything." Scott Cooper played for me...he was drafted by Boston in the third round. When Cooper was playing, we had tons of scouts. We would get out of school about 2:15 P.M. and I had my players get to the field by 2:30. When the visiting team would arrive, they could have the field when we were done. One day we're there early and we're taking batting practice. I see this slender black gentleman walking towards the field. I figured he was just another scout because they would always get there early. He comes up and says, "Coach, I'm up here to see Scott Cooper play. My name is Gene Baker, and I scout for the Pittsburgh Pirates." Gene Baker... man, that just blew my mind because when I lived in Chicago the Cubs had Banks and Baker. "Banks to Baker to Cavaretta"... it was a double play combo. He was one of my idols when I was in Chicago. The Cubs weren't my favorite team, but I watched all of their games. I was also a big **ERNIE BANKS*** fan. I was like, "Holy crap....Gene Baker!" So I told him, "Gene, you won't believe it!" And I started talking to him and he was like, "Is that

***ERNIE BANKS** became the first black manager—on an interim basis—in major league history after Cub manager Whitey Lockman was ejected in a May, 1973 game....Banks is an ordained minister and wed former Cub pitcher Sean Marshall and his wife....Banks and O.J. Simpson are cousins. Their grandfathers were twin brothers.

right?" We talked and BS'd and talked about Cooper for a little bit. He said, "Well, that's why I'm here, to see him play. I heard he's a great player."

The following year, we had another pretty good team and the scouts were coming around again, but I didn't see him. I asked one of the scouts, "Hey, where's Gene Baker?" They said, "Coach, he died. He passed away." I didn't know that at the time I met him, he already had cancer and was fighting it, but he had not said anything. That was a thrill that I got to meet him!

It's satisfying that maybe something you did helped a player move on. I felt all along that Cooper had a shot. I'm probably more proud of Scott now that he's here in St. Louis helping the St. Louis kids develop as players. He's working with them in the hitting clinics and sharing his tremendous knowledge. He's been coached by Williams, **YASTRZEMSKI***, Boggs and many great players that are part of the Boston tradition. He's got a lot to teach kids and I'm proud of the way he's developed as a person and for what he's done for the St. Louis area.

What's funny in baseball are the phrases... "hitting" or "pressing" or "loading the gun" or "throwing the bat at the ball." Well, Scott talked about "pulling down on the knob." I had never heard that before. I had never heard it expressed that way for as long as I have been in baseball. I would call it "throwing the bat at the ball." Sometimes a light will come on for a child with just one of those little catchphrases and it will suddenly come together for him. I played down in Missouri for a year with Hi Simmons and that was one of Simmons' things; "We don't swing at the ball in Missouri, we throw the bat at the ball." That's how I picked up on that phrase....

---

*A Carl **YASTRZEMSKI** model Louisville Slugger was the famous bat that Wendy Torrance (Shelley Duvall) used in the 1980 film, "The Shining"...to strike her husband Jack.

One year I get a call from Willie McGee. He said, "Hey Coach, what's the chances of me doing some work up at the cages at Pattonville High School?" He was living nearby in the Autumn Lakes subdivision. He said he didn't really want to be up at the school when a lot of kids were there. We had an activity bus that left at 5:00 pm and we didn't start our evening classes until 7:00 pm. I suggested, "Why don't you come out around 5:30. I'll set it up and have the custodians work it out with you. By the way, do you mind....I have a kid that's in the Cardinals organization—Scott Cooper—would you mind Scott being up there with you?" He said, "Oh no! That would be great!" Scott came to the high school to meet him, and I think that Willie was very instrumental to Scott. They worked well together and Willie had certain things to say while he was hitting. We had Bernard Gilkey, Cooper and Willie and then another kid...Charlie Hillemann, who was in the Padres organization. We had these three young kids up there with McGee—what an opportunity!

McGee had also asked if we had a pitching machine, and I said, "Yeah, but we got the wheel kind." Willie said "Well, do you mind if I bring up my arm machine?" Of course I told him to bring it on up later. Willie said, "Hey Coach, you guys go ahead and use it. I'm going to leave it here." Then Willie got traded . He called me up and said, "Hey Coach, you know that machine I left up there? Well, you guys can just keep it." So he donated it! I don't know if it's still up there or not. If it is, the people up there today probably don't even know that it was Willie's....

On the weekend when Al Nipper was getting married a lot of the players were coming into St. Louis because Al went to Hazelwood West—players like Roger Clemens and Mike Greenwell. Coop calls and asked, "Coach, any chance we can get up to the gym to shoot some hoops and throw the ball around a little bit in the gym on Saturday?" I said, "Ok, I'll set it up for you with the custodian." When I came in that next Monday, there was a ball on my desk signed by Clemens saying,

"Best Wishes Coach Benben, **ROGER CLEMENS***." That was really neat!...

I have seen a number of great Cardinals. I have seen Flood and I've seen a number of center fielders but I have a hard time thinking there's anyone better than Jimmy Edmonds. He showboated to a degree, but he was awfully good...Ted Simmons came to camp with his long hair, no cap, t-shirt hanging out, baggy shorts and flip flops. He gets in the cage, and he was amazing, "Whoomp!" He's just ripping the ball! I don't think that I've ever seen a player with faster hands than Ted Simmons...unbelievable even in flip flops!

I've had a really good time doing what I do. I've coached a lot of years and coached a lot of really good players. I try to keep coaching and being a fan separate, but it's hard because you always have an opinion, you're always critiquing. I was never a big LaRussa fan but I am a big Whitey fan. I could almost predict what Whitey was going to do, because that's what I would do. I would know about two innings beforehand what Whitey was going to do. With LaRussa, I would go, "Now why in the hell is he doing that?" LaRussa and I just never connected.

*In July 2007 Yankee starting pitcher **ROGER CLEMENS** was older than five of the retired Yankees who played in that day's OLD-TIMERS game.

DEEP THOUGHTS, CHEAP SHOTS, AND BON MOTS

A guy had been coaching my son in baseball since they were seven years old. We became good friends and are both Cardinal fans. A couple of times a year my Cubs friend and several others will go to Wrigley and a couple of times we go to Busch. A few years back, we were in the new Stadium. The game was over and there were 40,000 fans trying to leave the Stadium. We get down by Gate 3 and my Cub friend, Kevin Uphaul says, "Where's the bathroom?" I look across the heads of all these people and spot the M-E-N's sign. "It's straight across there, Kevin." He's gone forever. The people were thinning out. I look over and I saw the whole word, W-O-M-E-N. "I don't think I sent him to the right bathroom! He's not going to be very happy with me when he gets back."

We finally went outside and waited for him. He's a real low-key guy who doesn't get excited about anything. He comes out, "Thanks a lot for the nice directions!" I said, "Where have you been? It was right there!" He was wearing his Cubbie blues and trying not to ruffle any feathers.

He had gone inside the ladies room, looking straight ahead when he noticed a lot of stalls! He said, "I look over to my left, and look over to my right, and said, 'Hello, Ladies!' I had a dilemma because I was next! I paused and thought about it for a bit and thought it best if I just left. Nobody screamed or said anything, so I just left."

He found the Men's restroom and met us outside the Stadium. Of course, he's accusing me of doing that on purpose which I may or may not have done subliminally! He was the perfect guy to have that done to—a Cubs fan!

What had happened was, I really did think I sent him to the Men's room, but what I didn't realize is that as I looked across the concourse. I did see the word M-E-N, but the W-O proceeding it was blocked by a taller man to my left. I accidentally sent him to the Ladies room, although in retrospect, I don't regret it.

—Blaine Poland, car dealer, Effingham, IL

I grew up in Iowa, listening to Harry Caray doing Cardinal games on KMOX. It was a dream of mine when I started working for the Redbirds in the early 1960s. I was at Spring Training with the Cardinals in 1971 when Dan Devine was named the coach and general manager of the Packers. Dan, the former Missouri head coach, was a good friend of Bing Devine, my boss with the Cardinals (no relation). Dan called Bing and said he was looking for someone to come in and help him since he was doing both jobs. He wanted someone to be able to handle the contracts and paperwork so he wouldn't have to deal with it. Bing knew that I had gone to school at Marquette and was a big Packer fan. Bing told me that it would be a big jump in salary and jump-up in job description, so if I wanted him to, he would throw my name into the hat. I told him I wasn't looking to leave St. Louis, but that I would be interested in talking to them. Dan Devine flew down to St. Petersburg and interviewed me, then brought my wife and me to Green Bay a few days later and offered me the job. It happened very quickly. In Bing's later life, I would see him from time to time. Whenever he would see me, he would always say, "Don't forget, I'm the guy who got you that job"...because by that time I had become the President and Chief Executive Officer of the **GREEN BAY PACKERS**[*]. I was with the Packers for almost 40 years, 20 of those as President. I started with the Packers on June 1, 1971 as assistant general manager.

A lot of problems in Major League Baseball and professional football are very similar. Of course, the jobs I had were very different. With the Cardinals, I was in public relations

---

[*]Until the 1990's, the **GREEN BAY PACKERS** played half of their home games at Milwaukee County Stadium. Because of the park's baseball configuration, both NFL teams shared the same sideline.

which meant I was basically a friend to the players. In Green Bay, I was the guy who negotiated contracts so it was a different kind of relationship. As far as dealing with the player problems, stadium problems, financial problems and the like, the NFL and Major League Baseball are very similar. I've said one of the huge advantages of the NFL is they only play 16 games a year. Playing one game a week means that every game has playoff implications. It's tough to say that about other sports when they are playing 82 or 162 games a year. I cherish my time in St. Louis, and I'm still a Cardinal fan to this day.

—**Bob Harlan**, Green Bay, Wisconsin. Father of sports announcer Kevin Harlan and sports agent Bryan Harlan.

At the beginning of the 1983 season, after the '82 World Series, the Cardinals all got their World Series rings. It was the last game of a home stand and they were headed out on the road. George Hendrick gets his ring and says, "Here. Take care of this, will you?" because they were going to be gone for a couple of weeks. I said, "What do you mean?" He said, "We're going out of town, and I don't want to be hauling this thing around." For a month or so, I had George Hendrick's World Series ring. I wore it out to dinner a few times. I wasn't wearing it too much, but it sure felt good....

George Hendrick is a friend of mine, and he was managing in the Arizona Fall League a few years later. George invited me to sit in the dugout with him for a game. The Cardinals' top prospect then was Eli Marrero. Eli was a catcher. He ultimately played outfield and was probably a better position player there rather than catcher. I was in the dugout—not in uniform—but with George the whole time. Eli got injured in left field. He ran into the wall and hurt his shoulder. After every game, the manager has to file a report back to St. Louis. George and I spent about an hour and a half after the game trying to figure out how to report that Eli was injured in the game but not to report that he was injured in left field. George was worried that he'd get canned for playing the top catching prospect in the field! We craft this report that says Marrero sustained a shoulder injury.

It was factual but it never said he was playing left field or how he injured it. George didn't know how to write the report himself. He said, "You've got to help me write this thing. I don't want to tell them he was in the outfield...they'll fire me! He was not supposed to be an outfielder!"

—**Lewis Levey**, St. Louis business tycoon.

I grew up near Calvary and Bellefontaine Cemeteries in St. Louis. My good buddy, who I went all through grade school with, lived in the cemetery because his father was the caretaker for the Bellefontaine **CEMETERY***. They had a little private gate that led up to their house. There were no tombstones; there was just a field to the side and a lake in the back. His dad would keep that field clean and mowed, and we would play Indian Ball there. We set two markers up and would pitch, hit, and score runs. There were trees about three hundred feet away, so if you hit one out in the trees it was a home run. We called it the Bellefontaine Cemetery League!

Baseball has been a part of my life for a very long time. As a kid we could run the bases at Sportsman's Park....no lines to wait in like you wait today. You could just run the bases as much as you wanted—just get out on the field and go! What I liked most of all back then as a kid was standing in the batter's box trying unsuccessfully to stretch my legs apart so that I could fit my feet into the deep holes made in the dirt by the players during the game. What a challenge that was!

I went to the Cardinal tryouts at Sportsman's Park in 1947. I was sixteen years old at the time and took the Bellefontaine and Grand Avenue street cars to get there. For the tryout, all we needed to take was a glove and spikes—if you were that rich. I anticipated all sorts of things—running, hitting, sliding, catching. I thought that I could pass those tests, so I was ready!

---

*New Cathedral **CEMETERY** in Baltimore Maryland is the resting place for three Hall of Famers: John McGraw, Joe Kelley, and Wilbert Robinson.

Everyone was told to line up at the tables on the field and they pinned a number on your back with safety pins. It looked like they cut out old white t-shirts and put the numbers on them and pinned them on you. I was given the number "426." That was somewhat depressing to me. I had always envisioned me in a Cardinals uniform with a much lower number! Then I thought, somehow it was a sign from above! Do you know, at that time number 4 was the Cardinal shortstop Marty Marion, number 2 was Red Schoendienst, the second baseman, and the number 6, was Stan Musial, the first baseman. Here I am many years later and I still remember the numbers that were pinned on my back.

Back to the happenings of tryouts; the coaches broke us up into two groups by preferences for positions. I chose the outfield. After we gathered into the group, they took us out to right field and told us they were going to check our abilities to run, catch, and throw. As I looked around, some guys came in full uniforms and others were just in uniform jerseys and others, like me, were in some type of old white t-shirt. Some guys had upper arms as big as my thighs and seemed old...eighteen, nineteen and some even in their twenties.

They told us they would hit three balls towards us, one to go get and check on our running, two more to check on our throwing and accuracy. Those last two were not included in my anticipation list! As I waited for my turn, my hopes faded. There were guys one-hopping their throws to home plate. One guy even got four balls—they backed him to the wall and he still threw a one-hopper to the catcher. I'll never forget seeing that! He did drop one ball, and I thought that was going to be the opening that I needed. Then it was my turn. Oh boy...it was a "go get it ball!" I ran to it quickly...I could run pretty well in those days. Then I caught it and I fired it home. The throw wasn't too bad and neither was the distance. The second ball was over my head, but I still caught it, stopped and turned with all of my 145 pounds and threw it home flat-footed! It was the most beautiful rainbow that I could have produced.

I thought if I got it high enough, the wind would catch it and get the end result that I needed to impress the coach. I must have done pretty well because they hit me another ball, but unfortunately, the wind died and with it my career with the St. Louis Cardinals. The coach asked if I wanted to try out another position and I said, "No sir, Thank you. I'll just go back to playing cemetery ball." That seemed to confuse him! Good news though, my "426" may someday, hopefully, be retired in the one and only Bellefontaine Cemetery League where I played many, many games.

At my eightieth birthday, my kids threw me a huge party. They brought out my old number from when I had tried out for the Cardinals and retired it on my eightienth birthday! They had an official unveiling of my number 426, beautifully framed with the newspaper article from that long ago day containing a photo of a group of us who were there trying to make the team. It was so wonderful! I always knew it would be retired one day!

—**Don Dempski**, St. Peters, MO

Quite a few years ago, we played in the Cystic Fibrosis Jack Buck Golf Tournament that he had for years at Norwood Country Club. Jack knew me a little bit because my son has Cystic Fibrosis. We hit a ball on a green on our second shot. The putt wasn't too far away, maybe fourteen feet, and we were going for a birdie. Jack came over and said he wanted to putt with us. Jack put his ball down about four feet from the cup. He said,

"Everybody putts from here." Of course when he did that, I put my ball down, putted it in, as Jack walked away. If you ever play in his tournament, they always send one person with you that is a "spotter", to keep track of your score. When Jack left, I looked at the other guys that I was playing with wondering if we should put our ball back where it should have been or what? I then looked at the scorekeeper and shrugged my shoulders. The spotter said, "If Mr. Buck says it's a birdie...it's a birdie." So we just picked everything up and went on, laughing about it. I thought it was very funny and very nice of him.

In '98, Jack invited my son and I down to a game. We got their early, of course, and he took us on the field for batting practice. My son Donny got really excited because Jack was going to take him into the clubhouse before the game. They came back out and we were sitting in the dugout—my wife, my daughter and him. Donny was standing on the steps with a ball he wanted to get autographs on but nobody was around. Mr. Buck saw Donny standing on the steps. Jack waved Donny out onto the field. I don't really know what he said to him, but as soon as he told him...whatever it was...Donny took off for the batting cage, ran around and got everybody's autograph on the ball. He was just a little kid at the time. He thought that was just great!

Then we all went back and sat in the dugout until approximately fifteen minutes before the game started. Mr. Buck came out and took us up to the radio booth and talked to us for a little bit on the air before we went and sat down in our seats to watch the game.

Jack Buck was the best ever: the best announcer, the best person!

—**Don Hart**, Owner of Maryland Yards Restaurant,
Maryland Heights, MO

I grew up in Fayetteville, North Carolina. I was a St. Louis Cardinal fan as a kid, because I could get KMOX on my radio when I would go to bed. My parents thought I was sleeping, and I'd be listening to the Cardinal game. I was a big Harry Caray fan.

I almost played baseball instead of golf. Fortunately, I did make the right decision. When I went on the PGA Tour, any time we went to a city where there was a Major League ballpark, I would go to a game. In 1965, the World Series was the Dodgers and Minnesota. Bob Rosburg was a buddy of **DRYSDALE***, Koufax, and some other Dodgers. We went to a couple of games in Dodger Stadium. I met Mr. Kawano, who was the clubhouse manager for the Dodgers. He said, "When you go to Chicago, you have to meet my brother, he's your biggest fan." Leo Durocher was coaching at the time for the Dodgers. Then he became manager of the Cubs and, of course, I meet Yosh Kawano, the legendary Cubs clubhouse man, who became one of my closest, dearest friends. Because of Yosh, I'm now a Cub fan.

—**Ray Floyd**, 1976 Masters and 1986 U.S. Open Champ

When Walt Jocketty was General Manager of the Cardinals he was our next door neighbor in Richmond Heights. The whole Jocketty family were wonderful neighbors. One night, shortly before midnight, my daughter came running into my bedroom and says, "Mom! Mom! Wake up! There's a stranger trying to get into the house! He has a red Cadillac." I was wearing some pajama bottoms and an Old Navy shirt. I felt that an intruder would probably not be driving a red Cadillac. I went out into the foyer, and there standing in my house was a man that I had never met before...Tony LaRussa! LaRussa looks at me and says, "Whoops! I must be in the wrong house!" I said, "Are you looking for Walt Jocketty's house?" and he said, "Yes." I said, "It's right next door." He said, "Which way?" I pointed to the right. He turned around, got in his car and drove across our

---

*The late Buzzy Bavasi, when G.M. of the Dodgers, once offered his pitchers $25 if they would run a mile. Don **DRYSDALE** said he would do it right after Jesse Owens won twenty games...Drysdale once said that his most important pitch was his second knockdown pitch. "That way the batter knew the first one wasn't an accident."

lawn to the Jockettys' house. That's the only time I "met" Tony LaRussa.

—**Cathy Fayette**, Richmond Heights, MO

In our home, our bedroom is upstairs. We have a big semi-circle window above our foyer. There was a period of time that whenever we were in our bedroom, we would hear a clicking sound. We had no idea what was causing this clicking sound. We just blew it off as the house settling or perhaps a noise from outside, or maybe it was coming from the neighbors because we live in a condo. There was one particular morning that the clicking was louder than usual. We wondered again, "What is that noise?" Our room is a pretty good size so we were moving around, glancing out the windows, looking down the steps and looking through the hallways. We just couldn't figure out what it was. I went out into the hallway thinking that maybe it was the fire alarm. Any time the battery would go low it would make a beep sound so maybe that's the clicking. I stood there watching the fire alarm, but nothing was happening. I went back into the bedroom and suddenly, I hear it again. I looked in the bathroom to make sure it wasn't a faucet or sink. Finally, I looked out the window above our foyer. The window is shaped like a big half circle and sits about two stories above the ground. I see a cardinal bird hitting the glass. The bird would disappear for awhile and then "Click. Click. Click." The click was the bird's beak hitting the glass! At first, I didn't even realize it was a cardinal because it happened so fast. When I went out on the landing above our foyer, it wouldn't happen, but when I went back into our room away from the window, I would see the bird fly back up and hit the window again.

It finally dawned on me. I was always taught by my grandfather and my uncles that when you have a baseball or football jersey, you don't throw them on the floor, you don't crumple them up or stick them in a drawer. Whether clean or dirty, you always hang your jerseys. I had a hook, the kind that you would basically see on the back of a bathroom door or a fitting room over the top of our bedroom door.

Our bedroom door had a certain kind of lock on it. We had accidentally locked it one time and couldn't get in, so we had to bust a hole in the door to get the door unlocked. Until we got the door fixed, I would hang this jersey on the hook to cover the hole because it looked bad. Here's this authentic Cardinals jersey that I had gotten for my 30th birthday and was so proud. I always hung it up—dirty or clean—with the birds on the bat facing toward the window above the foyer. That cardinal bird saw those birds on the bat that were only a few feet away when the beak would hit that window. That bird was trying to get to those Cardinals on the bat on my jersey that was hanging on the hook over our bedroom door.

—**Bill Crotty**, Fairview Heights, IL

In 2002, out of the blue, I would get comments like, "You look like so-and-so." I think everybody likes to look like someone! When I was younger and had lots of hair, I would get Andy Van Slyke. When I got older and started thinning a little bit, I would get Will Clark. Then when I grew nasty facial hair people would say I looked like Mark McGwire. There was one friend of mine that told me I looked just like Rick White. Rick White was journeyman pitcher that played on eight or nine teams. He was a reliever that had his head shaved and had a physique like me too—he no longer had abdominals, he had baddominals! It was the first time I looked at a player and said, "Wow! He does look like me!" I wanted to get a picture of me standing next to him. Rick White was with the Mets in the World Series when I saw him. He actually got traded to St. Louis so I had to get a picture.

One night, after the game, we were sitting in the bar inside of the Marriott and in walks Mitchell Page, the hitting coach. He sits down at the table next to us. Initially, we weren't going to say anything to him, but he kept looking over at us. We were wondering why he kept looking at me. The young lady he was with asked, "Are you guys Cardinal fans? I can get you tickets." She said it would cost us $50. Mitchell Page looked at me and said, "It won't cost you anything. I'll get you tickets if you need them." We started talking and I was going to tell him how much I love that Renteria hits to right field. He stopped me, "I'm don't want to talk baseball!" We continue to talk and eventually he warms up and we start talking a little baseball. I told him, "I often get that I look like a player on the team." He looked at me and he said, "Who's that?" He is about to take a drink, and I told him, "Rick White." He snorted while drinking and his drink came out of his nose. He looked at me and was shaking his head and snickering. I took that as approval—that I must look like him. He wiped his lip and touched his nose and said, "If you put a jacket and tie on, you might get lucky tonight!"

I never got the picture with Rick White. He was signed as a free agent by the Pirates. The next year the Pirates were in town and we were down at the bar Paddy O's, just south of the Stadium. A lot of people meet there before, after, and even during the games. Some players frequently pop in there too. As we are standing outside the bar, cabs were picking up some visiting players as well as people who were leaving and were gathered around the corner.

We notice some ball players were walking down from the Stadium and getting into cabs. Here comes Pirate pitcher Rick White walking right towards me. He had a button up, soft shirt on—similar to what I was wearing. We made eye contact. He looked at me, and I looked at him and it was one of those things, "Darn! We look like each other!" We didn't say anything—we just looked at each other in a funny manner . As we walked passed him, my friend tapped me on the shoulder and said, "He knows you look like him!" and I replied, "I think he does." My friend said I should have blocked his path and started mimicking him! Some of our mannerisms were even the same. If he gave up a home run, he would tilt his hat over his face—something I would do too....

—**Craig Ball**, Maryland Heights, MO

The Cardinals made it look so easy! Why couldn't I catch? Why couldn't I throw? Why couldn't I bat? They'd get out there and it just looked so easy! I teach a course during our January term called "Baseball, A Story of American Culture." We look at "what is a culture?" and then "how is baseball a culture?" From that, I learned that the hardest thing to do in any sport is to hit a ball. My husband, Ron, comes in and teaches the physics of baseball. So, I thought, "No wonder I couldn't do it!" It makes you appreciate the ballplayers even more to know that what they make look so simple, is really not that easy! Of course, they do it every day.

We have a program on Lindenwood's television station, called "Books and Strikes." I had been on that show for about four years even before I started this class. It was all men doing it and someone got the idea, "Wouldn't it be great if we did some book reviews?" I belong to the Baseball Literature Association. When these guys were thinking, "Who could we get from the English department to talk baseball literature?" One of my friends said, "Oh yeah! Sue Tretter!" They responded, "A woman? Really?" What's up with these people? Why can't a woman know as much about baseball as a man? Just because I never played it...I did try!

—**Sue Tretter**, Maryland Heights, MO

Chapter Seven

THE LAST OF THE NINTH

And Prayin' For Extra Innings

HEY NOW, YOU'RE AN ALL-STAR, GET YOUR GAME ON, GO PLAY

SCOTT COOPER

Scott Cooper is a baseball hitting coach/instructor for All-Star Performance Baseball Camps and Clinics. He is the co-founder of the St. Louis Gamers which is a group of select baseball teams in St. Louis. Cooper is from St. Louis, and played six years in the Major Leagues including one year with the Cardinals.

Growing up in St. Louis, we didn't have a ton of money but my dad would take me to a Cardinal game whenever he could get tickets. In 1982, I came home one day and he had two World Series tickets hiding in his pocket! I'll never forget the feeling—I was going to see a World Series game! I was 13 at the time and was just getting into baseball and got to go watch them beat the Brewers. Then, I started growing, getting better and played baseball at Pattonville High School as a freshman. The scouts started coming around about the end of my sophomore year.

I got drafted by the Red Sox in 1986, and I wasn't quite sure what to think. It was the Boston Red Sox...I didn't know anything about them. I signed with Boston after my high school team won the State Championship. I went to Elmira, New York for a short season of "A" ball.

My first start was against the Yankees in '91 and was on ESPN. I look at the lineup and it has me replacing Wade Boggs, hitting third with Jack Clark hitting behind me. I'll never forget Clark coming up to me saying, "Hey, I need you to get on. I need a couple of RBIs tonight for an incentive!" I thought, "Wow! I watched this guy—one of my favorite players in the '80's and now I'm on the same team! Not only that…I'm hitting in front of him!" I ended up going 2 for 3 that night.

I made the Red Sox team in '92—they traded Boggs. I played three years there and averaged 120-130 games those years. I got to play next to Cal Ripken in both of those All-Star Games. The really cool thing is that I'm playing third, Ripken was playing short and Ozzie was on the other team. We were doing the All Star dinner the night before. My Dad was a big baseball fan. **ROBERTO CLEMENTE*** was his favorite. Tommy Lasorda sat down next to me and introduced himself to my dad. He said, "I've heard good things about your son!" I told him that my dad's favorite player was Roberto Clemente so Lasorda starts ripping off these stories about Roberto. It was the coolest thing ever! And then Ozzie came over and introduced himself to Dad. I'll never forget my dad—he just couldn't get any words out of his mouth. It was the first time ever in my life that my dad's been speechless. Here he's been watching Ozzie as a Cardinal and then all of a sudden, his son's playing against him in the All-Star Game. That was really cool!

I had arthroscopic surgery on my shoulder at the end of the strike-shortened season of '94. I got traded to the Cardinals who just wanted me to come down to spring training to see if I could throw. My arm felt great. The surgery was completely successful. In fact, my arm still feels great to this day! I couldn't get a hold of my parents after I got the call from the Cardinals—they were fishing down in southern Missouri on the St. Francois River. The drive from Ft. Myers, where the Red Sox train to St. Petersburg was a really emotional trip.

*The right field wall at PNC Park in Pittsburgh is 21 feet high in honor of the late Pirate Hall of Fame right-fielder **ROBERTO CLEMENTE** whose uniform number was "21".

Just being a HUGE Cardinal fan...playing amateur baseball here in St. Louis...going from one of the best organizations with Boston and then going to my hometown organization where I grew up in St. Louis was just so awesome. I'm sure it's the same everywhere, in every state, but you grow up watching your hometown team. From a child you see your home team as the best and everyone else—every other team—is WAY in second, no matter what! All of a sudden I'm going to be playing for them! It was very emotional. Now my mom and dad are going to watch me play with Ozzie! How crazy it is that a kid from Pattonville High School is now getting to play with the Cardinals? Being from St. Louis, it was just an unbelievable thing.

It was about 12 years of playing professional baseball....bits and pieces of seven years in the big leagues. Think of this. It's so many boys' dream come true. First, you make it to the Major Leagues, then you play in a couple of All-Star Games and have your locker next to **CAL RIPKEN***, Kirby Puckett and Dave Winfield. You really want to pinch yourself! Then you get traded and get to play with Ozzie Smith on your hometown team.

I wish every boy that ever played baseball could just one time, stand in a Major League uniform, listen to the National Anthem and run out on to the field. It's just the most unbelievable feeling in the world!

---

*<u>**CAL RIPKEN**</u> Jr. holds the all-time record for the hitting into the most double plays.... When Lou Piniella played minor-league baseball in Aberdeen, South Dakota, the team's batboy was Cal Ripken Jr.

DOWN AT THE CORNER
OF WHAT AND WHY

JIM HAMMOND

Jim Hammond owns Sports Image, a sportswear company headquartered in St. Charles, MO. Hammond and his family are active in the Pujols Family Foundation which seeks to help those living with Down Syndrome in the U.S. and to improve the lives of the impoverished in the Dominican Republic. Their 11-year-old son, Brett, has Down Syndrome.

In 2009, Brett participated in the fundraiser Step Up for Down Syndrome and was a top fundraiser. His prize included throwing out the first pitch in the 2011 Build-A-Bear giveaway day at Busch Stadium. Brett, having a big heart, donated it back to the Foundation for some other person to have this incredible opportunity.

In mid-July, 2010, we were called by Jen from the Pujols Family Foundation...She asked if our son, Brett, would be willing to throw out the first pitch at the August 1st baseball game for the Build-A-Bear Company. I explained to Jen that Brett had donated that first pitch back to the Foundation after he had won it for his contribution to the Step Up for Down Syndrome fundraiser, and asked if there was another child that they could give the first pitch opportunity to. Brett was the only name that came to her mind at that time. She insisted he throw out the pitch—that she had a sign from above. We finally agreed and Brett was honored to do it for her.

We only had a couple of weeks before the game. Build-A-Bear Company had given us five tickets to the game, and I decided to purchase an additional 35 tickets for the people who wanted to see Brett throw the pitch. It was a couple of days before the game when I went through the 40 tickets and picked out five for my family that I thought were going to be in the shade. It was a Sunday afternoon game, I don't do the sun well, and I knew it would be a long day for Brett. I wanted to make sure he wouldn't be out in the sun while he watched the game.

Albert was just great with Brett. They had been together a couple of times before, but he was just outstanding that day. As we left the field to get back to our seats, it was already the bottom of the first inning. It was a sold-out game that day. As we came up to our seats, I went in first to our row and sat down next to a young lady who looked to be in her mid to late 30s. She had five young boys sitting between her and her husband. When I sat down she said to me that her boys were excited we sat next to them because they recognized Brett as the boy who threw the pitch to Albert.

I was kidding with her and said, "Don't tell me all five of those boys are yours!" and she said, "No. four of them are and the other is my son's best friend." The boys ranged in age from about 2-12 years old. They were from Owensville, Missouri and hadn't been to a game in three years. I asked her if she picked that day because it was Build-A-Bear Day and all the kids would get a free Ozzie Smith bear. She looked at me and said, "No. We picked this game because it was the only game we could come to. Our 8-year-old son has leukemia. He was diagnosed when he was eighteen months old and it had gone into remission when he was four years old. We just found out that it is back. He had surgery and went through a month of radiation and he has this week off before starting chemo."

I looked down and noticed that Ryan (the 8-year-old little boy) had a bandana on underneath his cap. He had his head leaning on his brother's shoulder who was 12 at the time. We continued to talk and she told me that Ryan was so excited the night before; he had told her that he didn't mind that he had lost his hair this time because he looked just like Albert Pujols. He had a Make-a-Wish when he was two years old and they got to go to Disney World. Ryan told his mom that if he got a second Make-a-Wish, he would make it to meet Albert Pujols. That just broke my heart because I know they don't give Make-a-Wishes unless things aren't going well.

Brett was sitting on the other side of my wife, Shelly, and I called him over. I whispered in his ear that there was a pretty sick little boy there—would he want to give him his Albert Pujols first pitch ball to help make him feel better? Brett didn't hesitate. He reached into his backpack and pulled the ball out of his glove and went down—this was the amazing point to me because I didn't tell him which boy it was—he went down to Ryan and gave him the ball and also gave him the biggest hug. Ryan's dad, who was sitting five boys down, was just watching the whole thing because he couldn't hear anything we were talking about. He just busted out crying. Crystal, the mom, started crying. I started crying and she started telling me, "You can't do this. Albert signed that ball for your son. It's his first pitch ball." I said, "Ma'am, if that ball helps your son starting tomorrow, it's exactly where it needs to be."

Brett (left) and Ryan (right).

We exchanged information with the family and enjoyed our visit with them. Brett and Ryan seemed to click as if they had known each other their whole lives. On the way home, I just couldn't shake it especially with that game—Albert hit a home run...the Cardinals won...every time Brett's been on that field with Albert he's hit a home run. It was just a magical day—one of those perfect days.

I got talking to my wife because it didn't seem right to me that you would have to have a little boy fighting for his life a second time. It didn't seem right that you had to wish for a negative for him to meet his hero. We have some property with a lake on it. Shelly and I had been talking about doing a fun fishing tournament for family and friends just to put it to use. We hadn't used it as much for the previous two years. I just mentioned to Shelly, "Why don't we turn this fun fishing event into a fundraiser. Let's raise some money for Ryan and his family.

David Backes, who plays for the St. Louis Blues, came by my house to pick up some inventory a couple of days after Brett's pitch and wondered how it went. I told Backes how we met this family and the story about Ryan and about the fundraiser and trying to eliminate the negative part of getting to meet Albert. He immediately said, "Count me in!" David had a busy weekend that weekend too, so I told him, "If you can come out, why don't you come and fish with Ryan." The Blues won Friday night and played in overtime on Saturday...but David Backes was out there on Sunday at 8:30 A.M. and gave Ryan a two hour fishing lesson before the tournament started.

The friendship couldn't have come at a better time for these boys. Brett was nine and Ryan was eight when they met. Ryan has been on the infield twice now. He's in a small town, Owensville and his friends didn't know quite how to treat him. My son was at an age with his Down Syndrome where the boys still liked him at school, but they knew he was different. He didn't get included in a lot of things. This was described to me by Ryan's mom, "It couldn't have happened at a better time. The one thing that Brett does for Ryan is that he treats him as his friend...no different. The one thing Ryan does for Brett is that he treats him as his friend and that he's no different. They're doing what the other kids should be doing but aren't." It's been a great friendship and they've become part of our family.

We would go to the games and when Albert would come to bat, Brett would put his hands over his ears. People would question, "Why does he do that only when Albert comes to bat?" I'd tell them, "Because he's been to so many games where Albert has hit a home run, he knows the fireworks are going to go off, and he doesn't like fireworks!" When he first started talking, he would say, "Albert home run." Then it was "Albert, home run, fireworks!"

I wish that everyone could see Albert when he's at one of his events with these kids. You cannot believe it unless you see it. The love that he has for these kids is unbelievable! If it were up to him, he wouldn't have any media involved with any of his events. He was just amazing!

I hosted a Father and Son fishing tournament for the Foundation the day after Father's Day in 2011...it was the day Albert broke his wrist. He came directly from the orthopedic surgeon's office after finding out his wrist was broken so he could be with those kids. He's just amazing.

One night the Foundation had the Father/Son bowling event. In the game earlier that night, Albert hit a foul ball off of his foot, and he was having trouble walking. Instead of going lane to lane to greet everyone, they put three chairs in a room and each father and son came in and sat with Albert and got their picture taken with him. He sat there for three hours with a foot that was throbbing but he had the biggest smile on his face when he sees those kids! It's always about the kids...never about him. It's just been disheartening as a parent of a baseball fan to see Albert leave. I understand the business side of it but I didn't understand why it had to be so personal.

THESE 7 THINGS ARE THE 10 REASONS TO LOVE BASEBALL

DICK GUIGNARD

Dick Guignard, 80, is originally from Indiana but has always been a Cardinal fan. Guignard now lives in the St. Louis area and attends games with his son from Indianapolis.

The first time I saw the Cardinals uniform it honestly brought tears to my eyes. I was about seven years old. I couldn't believe the color...the red...the excitement. They had the knee length socks and the pants at the time and everything looked so neat. I loved the Cardinals uniform and I always will! I have seen a few games and I thought how plain the other uniforms were. The Yankees had stripes...okay, big deal! I would love to meet the guy that could design a better uniform for the Cardinals. There isn't one out there.

I just turned 80, and I can't afford to go to many games. I go to three or four games a year, when my son from Indianapolis comes to town and buys tickets. He buys me good tickets! He got me a ticket to the 2011 World Series—the tickets said $600.00! I had a heart attack the previous December, and I almost had a heart attack then! I wrote my son about a week after the World Series and said, "Rich, having you take me to the World Series game was so meaningful. I loved that game more than any game in the world! I am proud to be your father!"

If more fathers would take their sons to their game instead of finding fault with them or buying them a laptop computer, the love of baseball would be passed down more to the next generation. If more fathers could share this sport...not only with sons but also with daughters...to let them know the depth of the love they have for the game and for the Cardinals, maybe some of this would rub off on these younger kids. This is a little bit of that American thing that we have lost as a country. We've got to pass this on to our kids...the love of baseball.

We just watched a movie the other night, *"Money Ball"*...where the guy said, *"Yeah, they just hit the home runs, but this guy has a higher percentage for being on base!"* When I watched that movie, it almost brought tears to my eyes to think that some guy is aware of something else rather than the guy that can bash it out of the park. I remember some of these catches that Ozzie Smith used to make—he was diving parallel to the ground and would make the catch. Now if that doesn't get you excited, nothing will! Where did that guy get this talent? Some people just say, "Good catch." I just think of the talent that these players have and all of the hard work. I get excited about all of these minor things!

One of the beautiful things that still chokes me up is sitting down before the game starts and looking at that baseball field...how perfect it is ...to first base, to second, to home...how nice the grass is. For a long time, the Cardinals have had the Arch mowed into the grass behind second base. It is all breathtaking. When the stands start to fill, you notice the size of the crowd increasing; it's like building a puzzle and then all of a sudden, all of the pieces come together.

Baseball is still the most colorful sport. I like football. I like hockey. I even watch women's basketball. I love sports to the hilt! You will never see a more colorful team, a more joyful color to run out on that field than that of the Cardinals...never! I don't care if the game lasts for another hundred years. The Cardinals are the most colorful! I must pay St. Louis a compliment! They have great Cardinal baseball coverage. It's just a beautiful city for baseball. It's a baseball town. I don't know how much it means to other people, but I think it means alot. We become attached to these guys! Molina, he's like a son to me. Years ago, even though Musial is a little older than me... Musial was like my big brother.

I subscribe to the *St. Louis Post-Dispatch* and one of the first things that I do is take out the sports section and set it aside. I cut every article out in the paper and I'll put two or three days together and mail it to my son in Indianapolis because he loves the game and I love the game. My son has a great room with Cardinal shirts, Cardinal schedules, and Cardinal bats on the wall. I'm an artist and even drew pictures of a cardinal. If this doesn't look like the original cardinal that you see flying through the air, I'll eat crow!

About a week after the 2006 World Series, someone in the family had a small reunion in the park. My grandson was there with his baseball glove. He said, "Grandpa, do you want to play a little catch?" Well I'll tell you, the emotion that brings...that first throw of the ball from him...to watch his precious, half awkward way of throwing the ball...it was a great moment. Compare that to the guy that can throw his ball a hundred miles per hour and think in terms of a little guy. It must be amazing. Someday he could be up there. I'd like to know who **MUSIAL*** threw his first baseball to. What were the reasons, the conditions, under which he threw it? Who was the person who received it, and what he thought of Musial?

When I see certain numbers or when I hear a regular name like Boyer or White, Ken Boyer and Bill White always come to mind. When I see the name Slaughter, I want to look up that person to see if they're some relation to Enos Slaughter. When

---

*In the 12th inning of the 1955 All-Star game in Milwaukee, Yogi Berra complained to Stan **MUSIAL** that his feet were killing him. Musial told Berra to relax and that he would "get him out of there in a hurry." Musial homered to end the game.

I see a number of a particular man that I liked, such as the number 9, I think of Enos Slaughter. I noticed that so many great ball players are left-handed: Enos Slaughter, Stan Musial, Lance Berkman. When I was at the supermarket yesterday, I noticed the guy in front of me was left-handed. I was joking around and said to him, "I noticed that you are left-handed. Would you please tell me where you were when the Cardinals were looking for left-handed pitchers?" For some reason a left-hander, right away, brings baseball to my mind.

My son and I have only gone to a couple of games this year because he's been wrapped up in his business, which is good but sad. If he were in another job, he would be home several times during the summer to take his mom and dad to a game, but he can't. When one of his customers gave him tickets to the World Series, he jumped on the phone and said, "Dad, I've got a surprise for you"...and he only got the tickets twenty minutes prior to that.

Game 6 in 2011 was miraculous...one in a million...we know that! That was one special World Series! I don't think at my age that I will see another one as exciting! We did it!

IF LIFE WAS FAIR THERE, WOULD BE NO WHEELCHAIRS

JULIEANN NAJAR

Julieann Najar lives in Spanish Lake in north St. Louis County. During the 2009 All-Star Game, several civilians were nominated and voted on to represent "every-day" All-Stars. Najar was the St. Louis Cardinals' representative. Najar started the not-for-profit organization, A Soldier's Wish List, when her son was called to serve overseas. He is now wheelchair-bound. Through her agency, civilians can "adopt" soldiers, sending them letters or care packages

I was nominated by my son for the civilian All-Star to represent St. Louis during the 2009 All-Star Game at Busch Stadium. When they started voting on the person to represent the St. Louis Cardinals, I had no idea that it was going to be as big as it was. I was shocked! The news of my nomination was sent out to a lot of our troops in Iraq and Afghanistan, and they were the ones that got me elected. People were going on their computers in Afghanistan and all over the world and voting for me to win. I know a chaplain in Iraq and he and the troops with him were doing a lot of voting too. When we got the phone call that I won...I had no idea! I was really flattered.

We were allowed to take someone with us to the All-Star festivities. Like I said, my son nominated me so I wanted to take him but he had been stationed in Iraq and was injured. He had a traumatic brain injury and also has progressive MS now so the heat would have been too hard for him. Instead, one of my friends, whose son is one of our soldiers who was in Iraq, went with me. We were picked up in a limo and were driven down to the hotel. I have never run so many places in two days—the Cardinals had us going all over. We were treated like such celebrities. It was really very nice.

Before the actual game, when we were waiting in line, Yadi Molina came up to us and said "hi"! I also told a player that I recognized him from an Avon commercial—it ended up being Derek Jeter. I was so taken aback when we did go out on the field! I was right in the front row and to hear all those people screaming and cheering...and knowing it was because of what we do...it was awesome! We had no idea that we'd be standing on the field with all the MLB All-Stars. These guys were phenomenal! I'm going to start crying.

While we were on the field, there was this very tall player who tapped me on the shoulder. I didn't know who it was at the time, but later found out it was Justin Verlander. He was so tall! He was so nice and told me to get in front of him because I was too short to see! When the players were greeting the civilians who were on the field, the little Japanese guy, Ichiro Suzuki—you could tell he was very embarrassed and very unsure of himself. Being from Hawaii, I know a bit about the culture so I just said to him "Arigatou". He starts speaking fluent Japanese to me, and I have to say, "Oh! No, no, no! I'm so sorry—that's all I know!" So he bowed, and I bowed. The player that really impressed me, though, was Mark Buehrle. He came up and tapped me on the shoulder. He said he wanted to give me a hug because he was so impressed with what our agency does for the troops, and he really liked it! I was so taken aback by his kind words—it really meant a great deal to me. He said something like, "Give me a hug for good luck!" The week after that, he had a no-hitter!

The other guy that was really nice was Ozzie Smith. I had previously done an interview with him. When we were coming in from the field, he yells, "Julie! Julie! Remember me?" Oh my gosh...he remembered me! He was such a nice guy and just made me feel like we were the stars that day!

SOMETIMES GOD JUST HANDS YA ONE

MIKE SELBY

Mike Selby and his wife Jill live on a farm near the town of Welton, Iowa. Welton is home to Buzzy's Tavern, which is world famous all over Welton. Mike Selby and his brother Mark have been known to leave work at noon, drive non-stop three hundred miles to St. Louis, go to a Cardinals game, hop in their car and drive back the same evening, get two hours sleep and show up for work in the morning.

We became Cardinal fans because my mom was a big fan. She was a nut! My dad didn't pay much attention to it. We never went to a lot of games when we were kids; we were farmers and didn't have much of a chance to get down to St. Louis. As we got older, I was able to take my boys more than my folks ever took me. We were blessed with two sons: Chad and four years later, Cory.

In 2000, Jill, Cory, Chad, and Mike Selby

Cory was very much an autographer! He loved to chase players the entire weekend of Winter Warm-Ups. In 2001, he bought himself a bat—a George Hendrick game-used bat. He got over 50 autographs on it that weekend of all different players. The biggest autograph was Albert Pujols. The neat thing about the Albert autograph is that he signed it "Albert Jose Pujols." No one knew who Pujols was at that time, so we were able to go back in line three times. We got several autographs from him. Cory didn't pay for one of the autographs on that bat!

No doubt, Jim Edmonds was his favorite player because he was Mr. Hustle. In the summer of 2000, Cory's picture was taken getting the autograph of Jim Edmonds. You could see in his eyes, "Wow! I got my favorite ballplayer's autograph!" He got it on the sweet spot of the baseball! It was a Cardinal's Kids Crew Autograph Day at the Stadium. He was so excited!

Mike Selby and Cory Selby with Jim Edmonds at Cardinals Winter Warm-up, 2001

That summer, Cory was 15 years old and was at the Lutheran Church Youth Convention in New Orleans. On July 28, 2001 our world crashed. One of the counselors called us first—thinking Cory just fell down the steps. Then our pastor called and said,

"It's worse than that...it's not good. You better start praying." We didn't know it, but he had a congenital heart condition. He was waiting for an elevator with some of his friends after the opening ceremonies at the hotel when he decided to take the stairs. He was running up the steps at the hotel and collapsed. They couldn't get his heart back going the way it should be and he passed away right there on the steps.

I don't get *Gameday Magazine*, but my good Cardinal friend, Scott Steffens, does. Eight months after the funeral, Scott called and told me I better come look at the newest copy of *Gameday*. I went into town to look at the magazine. In a special pull-out section in the magazine for Cardinals Care there was the picture of Cory getting his baseball signed by Jim Edmonds. I took the magazine home to show my wife, Jill. We both thought there was a Higher Power at work—what was God trying to tell us. It was part of the healing process, I think.

In 2004, the year Cory was supposed to graduate high school, we gave each one of his classmates a ten dollar bill to "pay it forward"—to do something nice for someone else. There are 130-150 students in graduating classes at Central High School in DeWitt, Iowa. They have an awards ceremony at the end of the school year. We have continued it for ten years and counting.

A church in Clinton—about 30 miles away—got wind of this and asked Jill to give a talk one Sunday. When she got done, they asked us to pick a charity to make a donation to in lieu of payment. We told them if they did that, we wanted them to send it to Cardinals Christian Family Day. We picked that organization because the three things that were most important in Cory's life were God first—he loved working with kids in Sunday School, his family and he always loved the Cardinals. Those were the three things that Christian Family Day represented—the three things that Cory loved the most. They sent the money down to this group, and it was not long after when Judy Boen called us and wanted to know more about Cory and his story. She was the President of the Christian Family Day Organization. They decided they wanted to make Cory the 2005 Christian Family Day honoree.

From there, the Christian Family Day people invited us down to the game. We started passing the word along and we ended up with over 200 neighbors and friends going the 600 miles round-trip to Busch Stadium. Everybody had to buy their own tickets but we still had over 200 people. Everyone drove down themselves. There were no buses. The Millennium Hotel gave our group a discounted rate on rooms. Pretty much everyone stayed overnight. They gave us a big conference room to use, and we all sat together in the Stadium.

Chad Selby in center field with Jim Edmonds.

On Christian Family Day at the ballpark, they would have nine people—usually children—go out and stand by each of the nine players in the field during the National Anthem. We asked Judy if Chad could go out to centerfield with Jim Edmonds, hoping Jim played that day. Once again, God was on our side. Chad went out to centerfield and stood with Jim, and we were able to get some nice pictures of Edmonds and Chad talking as they were standing in the field. Of course, Chad took the picture of Cory with him and had a chance to tell Jim a little bit about it. I can remember Chad saying, "Jim told me if I needed anything else signed to just bring it down in the dugout." He would sign anything we wanted him to sign, but we just had him sign the picture...that was all. They sat and talked quite a while. Chad was the last one out of there. It was definitely a good moment for Chad, I know.

After the game, Edmonds and Abraham Nunez asked us to come down to the dugout, so the three of us got to go down in the dugout. That was pretty special. This little lady came over to my wife. Jill didn't know who it was, but it was Deidre Pujols. She said, "Would you like to meet my husband." She took us around the corner and down a little chute and he and Nunez were sitting there. She said, "This is my husband, Albert." We got a picture with Albert and our family. That was special...

The high school kids that have received the money have just done so many nice things. We hear some good stories from the "pay-it-forward" awards. There was one boy that took the ten dollars and took two other young kids that wouldn't be able to go to a game down to a River Bandits game, the Cardinals Class A team until recently. One boy took our ten dollars and added his money with it to aid a family in need. Kids buy flowers for their grandmas in nursing homes. One young man said he was in a convenience store when a woman came in who didn't have any money for gas. So he gave her the ten dollars still folded up in his wallet.

Mike and Chad Selby at Cardinals Christian Family Day

By helping other people, Cory is still helping others here on earth. He lives on...we've never wanted to forget Cory. If you ever met him, you wouldn't forget him. He had such a contagious smile! God won't let us forget our son—there is always a hole in our hearts. Recently, a friend gave me a great perspective. He said, "If God had come to you twenty five years ago and said to you, 'I'll give you a healthy, happy, terrific son named Cory...a kid that will share your family values, faith and love of the Cardinals for 15 years and then I take him back. Deal or no deal?"

Thank you, Lord.

ALL IT TAKES IS ALL YOU GOT

BRIAN MCGILL

Brian McGill is with IAA Credit Union in Bloomington, Illinois. After growing up in Mount Zion, Illinois, he graduated from Eastern Illinois University and moved to Bloomington where the Cub fans outnumber the Cardinal fans about 60% to 40%.

Back in 1982, the day before the Cardinals came back to St. Louis trailing Milwaukee in the World Series 3-2, my friend, Greg Spain, was able to get a hold of a pair of tickets to Games 6 and 7 at Busch Stadium. He called and offered me the chance to go to one of the games or both. The price was $50 each which was a good deal but I had just emptied my meager bank account for a down payment on a new car and payday was still a week away. I told him I would take the ticket to Game 7. I figured that would give me an extra day to scrape up the money and if I was going to get a chance to attend the World Series, why not go with the opportunity to see the Cards win it all.

The night of Game 6, I was at my grandparents' house preparing to watch the game with my grandfather. Like many children, I had grown up listening to the Cards on KMOX with a grandparent. My grandfather would rather listen to the game on radio than watch on TV. The only exception was when the Cards were in the World Series. He would still have the radio on but would also follow along on television.

Before the game and during the long rain delays in the game, I would go in the kitchen and make some phone calls to try to round up at least $50 needed for the ticket to Game 7. I called everybody I knew and offered to sell about everything I had.

I was having no luck in coming up with the cash. I'm sure my grandmother heard some of my conversations and told my grandfather about what was going on. As the night wore on and it became apparent that the Cardinals were going to play for the championship the following evening, reality set in that I was not going to see this game.

I had exhausted all my resources for extra money. The game ended and I was preparing to leave when my grandfather came over to me and handed me a crisp $100 bill. He told me, "I've been to the World Series and seen the Cardinals in the World Series. Now, it's your turn. It's an experience you will never forget." I don't remember exactly what I said to him but I can remember the salty taste of tears as I babbled something.

The next day Greg and I headed down to the St. Louis early in the afternoon from our home in Decatur, Illinois. It was about a two hour drive and we were determined to get there and soak up as much of the atmosphere as possible. Greg had been to the game the night before and had soaked up more than atmosphere. He had a case of the "brown bottle flu". So, he was a little less excited than me but not much.

We listened to KMOX on the trip and remembered Jack Buck commenting on the cold weather expected by game time. He said if the Cardinals were winning you won't notice, but if they fall behind, it's going to get mighty chilly. When we got just south of Collinsville, Illinois on I-55, we caught sight of the Goodyear blimp hanging above downtown St. Louis. That's when it hit me that I was going to an extraordinary event. After parking the car and heading over to the Stadium, our senses were assaulted by jazz bands, blues bands and rock bands as well as ticket scalpers. We were offered $300 a piece for our tickets in section 330. This was very tempting considering that the night before I had only a few bucks in my pocket. Greg and I both decided that the money would be spent in a short time but the memory would last forever. Besides, my grandfather wanted me to be at this game. So, selling the ticket was never really an option.

Once inside Busch Stadium it seemed like the sights and sounds were not real. Growing up and watching the World Series on television really doesn't do it justice. Everything is louder, brighter and bigger when you attend it the first time. What you probably notice more than the sights and sounds is the feeling inside the ballpark. It's a combination of the excitement of just being there coupled with the nervousness of that's your team actually playing in the World Series. Game 7 begins and the Redbirds fall behind by the middle innings. By the fifth inning, Greg and I agreed that true to Jack Buck's comment, it was indeed mighty chilly weather. Then Keith Hernandez ties the game with a single that from our section looked like it would never drop in safely. George Hendrick puts the Birds ahead in the next inning and things are getting much warmer in the park.

As the ninth inning rolls around we take a look at the Stadium. There are people standing at the exit ramps poised to charge the field. A fan is straddling the right field wall as Bruce Sutter prepares to pitch to Gorman Thomas. With each pitch, the fan gets closer to falling over onto the field. George Hendrick keeps looking nervously over his shoulder at this guy to make sure that George can get away from him quickly in case the fan runs at him. When Sutter fans Gorman Thomas to end the game, Greg and I just stared at the field. We were in complete shock. I don't think we even spoke to each other for several minutes.

Just watching the scene unfold in front of us left us speechless—fans charging the field, players hugging and jumping, then running for their lives to the clubhouse. We watched for a few more minutes then decided to head down and join the party. On the way, Greg reached for one of the red, white and blue bunting banners hanging over the façade. A police officer drew his night stick and told him, "Don't even think about it."

We reached the field box level and climbed over the Commissioner's Box to get onto the field. The Box was totally demolished. The walls were broken down so all you had to do was step out and you were on the turf. I don't know how many people we joined out there but it was a lot. One guy had a pocket knife out and was trying to carve pieces of the **ASTROTURF*** out around the bases paths. A man in the outfield was trying to rip the turf up by the seams. He had it wrapped around his arm like a fireman carrying a hose. I had a plastic souvenir cup and went to all the base paths to scoop up dirt and then slide on them. A few more minutes passed and then the police department began to get their canine units out and clear the field. We felt that was our cue to leave.

We stopped on the way back up from the box seat section and glanced back at the field. Most of the crowd had been cleared by this time. The turf looked like it had been bombed. There were holes everywhere around the infield and parts of the outfield. It was a depressing sight knowing that the field would never look the same. When we got outside the Stadium, people were celebrating at every corner. We stayed and took in all the sights for several hours. Our most vivid memory was not of celebrating but came when we were leaving St. Louis. As we pulled back on the Poplar Street Bridge about 1 A.M. to head back north over the Mississippi, all we could see were headlights coming into the city for about four miles. The party was just beginning.

The following evening I went over to visit my grandparents and recount all that we had seen. I'll bet I talked non-stop for several hours. Grandma and grandpa just listened and grinned.

*An announcer once asked Tug McGraw about the difference between **ASTROTURF** and grass. Tug replied, "I don't know. I have never smoked Astroturf."... When Monsanto told Judge Roy Hofheinz, the owner of the Astros, what they were going to charge him for Chemgrass (Astroturf), the Judge said, "That's amazing! That's exactly what I was going to charge you for the marketing opportunity!"

Okay it's not an infomercial but there a sequel to this book that you just finished...and that sequel will be available almost immediately.It's a fundraiser for a wonderful charity called Horizons For The Blind.

For full information on how to order the new book go to Horizons-blind.org. The book will be available in download-able form (Kindle, Nook, iPad), etc., audio and hard-cover. A limited number of the hard-cover books can be autographed and personalized by the author (Limited by the number the old coot can sign before he keels over).

The new book is titled *If Baseball's a Religion Why Don't the Cubs Have a Prayer?* The format will be the same and the main feature will be full-page reproductions of every *Sports Illustrated* with the Cardinals on the cover!

There's no credit check, there's no qualifying, it's a doozy!!!... Plus,it's a great way to launder twenty-five bucks.

YOU CAN BE A STAR!!

We hope that you have enjoyed *A Lotta People Are Cub Fans 'Cause They Can't Afford World Series Tickets*. Due to space and time considerations over 30 Cardinal fans with great stories could not be included.

Their stories...far better than the lousy ones in this book...will be included in *If Baseball's a Religion, Why Don't the Cubs Have a Prayer?"*

If you have a neat Cardinals' story, contact us today by email at printedpage@cox.net. Pay attention to this next line... we might have a pop quiz later. Please please, pretty please PUT CARDINALS FANS IN THE SUBJECT LINE AND YOUR PHONE NUMBER TOO...or just call the author directly at 602-738-5889. He'll probably answer...he's a lonely old man with no friends and a lotta time on his hands.

NOTE: NO ACTUAL CHICAGO CUB FANS WERE HARMED IN THE MAKING OF THIS BOOK!!!

Other Books by Rich Wolfe

For Cardinals Fans Only—Volume I
Remembering Jack Buck
I Remember Harry Caray
Ron Santo, A Perfect 10
Jeremy Lin, The Asian Sensation
For Cubs Fans Only
For Cubs Fans Only—Volume II
For Notre Dame Fans Only—
   The New Saturday Bible
Da Coach (Mike Ditka)
Tim Russert, We Heartily Knew Ye
For Packers Fans Only
For Hawkeye Fans Only
I Love It, I Love It, I Love It (with Jim Zabel, Iowa announcer)
Oh, What a Knight (Bob Knight)
There's No Expiration Date on Dreams (Tom Brady)
He Graduated Life with Honors and No Regrets (Pat Tillman)
Take This Job and Love It (Jon Gruden)
Remembering Harry Kalas
Been There, Shoulda Done That (John Daly)
And the Last Shall Be First (Kurt Warner)
Sports Fans Who Made Headlines
Fandemonium
Remembering Dale Earnhardt
I Saw It On the Radio (Vin Scully)
The Real McCoy (Al McCoy, Phoenix Suns announcer)
Personal Foul (With Tim Donaghy, former NBA referee)

For Yankee Fans Only	*For South Carolina Fans Only*
For Red Sox Fans Only	*For Clemson Fans Only*
For Browns Fans Only	*For Oklahoma Fans Only*
For Mets Fans Only	*For Yankee Fans Only—Volume II*
For Bronco Fans Only	*For Mizzou Fans Only*
For Michigan Fans Only	*For Kansas City Chiefs Fans Only*
For Milwaukee Braves Fans Only	*For K-State Fans Only*
For Nebraska Fans Only	*For KU Fans Only (Kansas)*
For Buckeye Fans Only	*For Phillies Fans Only*
For Georgia Bulldog Fans Only	

All books are the same size, format and price.
Questions or to order? Contact the author directly at 602-738-5889.